GREEK MYTHS

GREEK MYTHS

Tales of Passion, Heroism, and Betrayal

By SHOSHANNA KIRK

Illustrations by TINOU LE JOLY SENOVILLE

CHRONICLE BOOKS

SAN FRANCISCO

Library of Congress Cataloging-in-Publication Data available.

ISBN 0-8118-4306-8

Manufactured in Singapore.

Designed *By* AYAKO AKAZAWA
Typesetting *By* JANIS REED

Distributed in Canada *By* RAINCOAST BOOKS
9050 Shaughnessy Street
Vancouver, British Columbia V6P 6E5

10 9 8 7 6 5 4 3 2 1

CHRONICLE BOOKS LLC
85 Second Street
San Francisco, California 94105

www.chroniclebooks.com

. . .

Page 2:   APHRODITE, GODDESS OF LOVE.
Page 5:   HERACLES AND THE THESPIAN LION.
Page 6:   ARIADNE ABANDONED AT NAXOS.

CONTENTS

INTRODUCTION

Thousands of years after their inception, what is it about the myths of the ancient Greeks that still captivates us?

Greek myths are a celebration of humanity. They probe every human emotion, evoking laughter, pity, scorn, envy, disgust, hope. Gods and heroes alike remind us of ourselves—our weaknesses, our worst fears, our secret desires. Greek myths recount all the passions and fallibility of humans and remind us of the power of Fate, that seemingly illogical force that rules our lives. Testimony to the immensity of human creativity and imagination, Greek myths allow us to meditate what it means to be human and help us to recognize the continuity of that experience through the centuries.

The myths here are organized according to themes that touch the core of all of us; with familiar tales balanced with ones you might not know. What you'll find here is not the "definitive" version of each myth, for myths were never written in stone but were malleable, ever changing stories, transmitted orally or visually and only later written down. In antiquity, a myth may have possessed many variants, and as it evolved over the years in different parts of the Mediterranean world, it might have contained entirely different characters or different episodes. Myths were told and retold by Greek storytellers such as Homer and Hesiod, by classical philosophers such as Plato and Aristotle, by Roman poets including Ovid and Virgil, and by ancient mythographers (historians of myth) such as Apollodorus. The stories here, tales that could be rendered a thousand ways, mainly follow the original Greek sources. But because much of what we know of Greek myths has been shown to us through Roman eyes, I also consulted Roman texts. At times, I consulted lesser-known sources, too—obscure ancient authors or collections of fragments—for sometimes they provide surprising variants.

Greek myths are not fair or feminist. Though they often feature powerful, strong women, they are also replete with rapes and miserable marriages. Though they tell tales of justice, they also tell stories of the fury that can eat men's souls. In all these myths, human lives are determined not by the actors themselves but by Fate; choices are influenced and even destined by the gods.

Greek myths allow us to contemplate our humanity without asking us to question our own canons of belief—our own stories of gods, immortality, fate, and faith. Whereas we may not be able to appreciate our own culture's myths as fictional, most everyone today can appreciate the storytelling of Greek myths. (It's worth noting that myths were not necessarily swallowed as literal truth by the ancients, either. By the classical period, [480–330 BC], philosophers had begun to rationalize myths as allegories; Plato [428–346 BC], for example, advocated rejecting them wholesale.)

Nevertheless, since antiquity, humanity has returned to these myths again and again. They were revisited in word and image by the Romans, who though they conquered the Greeks, remained their most fervent admirers. For the educated of the Renaissance, learning about the Greeks and their myths, often through the lens of Roman art and literature, was the mark of erudition and good taste and signaled a departure from the Church. Hellenism, or love of things Greek, grew in the eighteenth century with the dawn of modern archaeology. The late eighteenth century and the nineteenth century witnessed neoclassical art and architecture that drew on Greek forms: Think of the White House or Monticello, Thomas Jefferson's Virginia plantation. Today, we bemoan the Sisyphean toil of working life, we search for our competitor's Achilles' heel, and we diagnose Oedipal complexes. We utilize the Greek myths to suit our own cultural needs: Freudian psychology of sexual impulses, Jungian interpretation of the collective unconscious, feminist deconstruction of gender roles.

These can all be meaningful ways to explore Greek myth, but here I ask you to simply enjoy. For the Greeks were wonderful storytellers, and these are some of their most engaging stories.

A NOTE TO THE READER

If you're coming to Greek mythology for the first time, or if you have only vague recollections from school, you might find keeping track of characters daunting. The unfamiliarity of the names makes them difficult to remember, and figures might make repeated appearances in different stories. To further complicate things, gods and goddesses have different epithets, additional names that describe them. Hermes, roughly equivalent to the Roman god Mercury, might be called Hermes *psychopompos* ("guide of souls," for the messenger god led the dead to the Underworld) or Hermes *Argeiphontes* ("killer of Argos," for he slew a monster named Argos). It's the same Hermes, but his different aspects are emphasized in different contexts.

To help you keep track of the rather overwhelming cast of characters, I've included an index as well as a conversion table listing Greek gods and heroes and their Roman equivalents.

THE MYTHS

CUNNING

ODYSSEUS AND THE CYCLOPS

First, I will tell of Odysseus, cunning Odysseus, who lost his way back home to Ithaca after the Trojan War . . .

Not long after he left Troy, Odysseus and his crew spotted a wooded island. They planned to anchor, find some food onshore, and enjoy some peace and quiet. They didn't know the island was home to the Cyclopes, one-eyed monsters that lived in caves, eschewing government and laws, and whose crops grew from rain sprinkled by Zeus (for, long ago, the Cyclopes had helped Zeus win a battle against the Titans).

Odysseus chose twelve of his crew to explore the island with him and commanded the rest to remain on board the ship, seated at the oars. Spotting one of the island's stange inhabitants, he and his men hurried to follow it, taking with them a wineskin filled with unmixed wine. Though the creature appeared monstrous, Odysseus wasn't afraid, for it was the law of Zeus that visitors should be welcomed and given a guest-gift by their host; certainly this creature would take pity on such a bedraggled set of travelers returning home from war.

While the Cyclops tended his flocks of sheep and goats, Odysseus and his men sneaked into its cave to wait for it. The cave was musty and filled with baskets of cheeses and pens crammed with bleating lambs and kids. Milk pails were strewn across the ground. A pile of willow branches in the corner appeared to serve as a bed.

The longer they waited, the more nervous Odysseus's companions became. "Let's just take some cheese and leave," they suggested. "We can always come back later to take a few lambs."

Odysseus told his men to stop complaining and be patient: He wasn't going to leave until he'd seen about that gift.

The men sighed and rolled their eyes. But trusting Odysseus, they built a fire and ate cheese and waited for the return of the Cyclops.

When Polyphemus, for that was the Cyclops's name, returned, he drove his fat ewes into the cave and rolled a huge boulder in front of the entrance. He didn't address Odysseus until he'd finished milking his ewes.

"Who are you, lurking there in the corner of my cave?" bellowed Polyphemus. "Some kind of pirates?"

"We are Achaean soldiers returning home from Troy," explained Odysseus. "We were blown off course, and Fate has landed us here. We come to you in supplication that you might give us a gift, as Zeus himself decrees."

"Sorry fool!" Polyphemus roared. "We Cyclopes don't care about Zeus's laws! What I care about, Achaean, is this: Where have you beached your ship?"

As Polyphemus spoke, Odysseus's men despaired, for they realized just how monstrous a creature he was. But wily Odysseus thought quick. "You see," he replied, clearing his throat, "the problem is that we have no ship. Poseidon destroyed it. We were the only ones to survive the shipwreck."

Before Odysseus could continue his fib, Polyphemus grabbed two men and smashed their skulls upon the ground and cut them up for his dinner. Then he ate them, entrails, flesh, and bone—every last bit—and when he'd finished, he lay down on his bed of branches and went to sleep.

Odysseus charged at the Cyclops, sword in hand, but stopped midway across the cave, remembering the boulder that barred their exit. It wasn't a rock of ordinary proportions: It was a veritable hunk of mountain. Odysseus and his men would never be able to move it on their own. So he put down his sword and contemplated how best to escape the Cyclops's cave.

When the Cyclops awoke, he grabbed two more men, smashed them upon the ground, and prepared them for breakfast. Then he led his fat flocks out to herd, rolling the boulder across the exit to the cave to trap Odysseus and his remaining companions.

While his men wailed in despair, Odysseus crafted a plan. Polyphemus had left behind a huge olive wood log, which Odysseus commanded his men to sharpen with rocks and harden in the fire.

When the Cyclops returned, he milked his ewes and prepared his grisly feast, snatching another two men, bashing their heads on the ground, and dining on raw flesh. After the Cyclops's dinner, Odysseus presented the creature with a bowl of unmixed wine (for only barbarians do not dilute their wine with water). Polyphemus greedily gulped it down.

"If you tell me your name," spat Polyphemus, "I will give you a gift."

Odysseus nodded, smiling. At last, the guest-gift! He gave the Cyclops another bowlful of wine. After drinking it, again the Cyclops asked his name, but again Odysseus refilled the bowl in silence. Only when the Cyclops's brain had been thoroughly marinated in wine did Odysseus speak:

"You ask my name? Nobody is my name. Everybody—all my friends and family—calls me Nobody."

"Well, then, Nobody," Cyclops replied with a belch, "here's my gift to you: I'll eat you last of all!" With that, he passed out on the dirt floor, vomiting wine and human flesh in his slumber.

Odysseus and his men took their olive stake out of hiding and heated it in the fire till the sharpened tip glowed hot. Taking a running start, they heaved the spike

into the monster's single eye and whirled it round and round until the roots sizzled and blood boiled out of the socket. The monster cried out and wrenched the giant splinter free, calling out for help from the other Cyclopes who lived nearby. When they arrived outside the cave, groggy from having been woken up, they shouted in to Polyphemus, "What do you want? Surely nobody is killing you by force or treachery?"

Polyphemus roared, "Yes! Nobody is killing me by force and treachery!"

There was whispering outside the cave. "Well, if you are alone, you must have some sort of madness sent by the gods. You would do well to pray to Poseidon."

Hearing his fellow creatures depart, the Cyclops roared. He tore the boulder from the doorway and blocked the exit with his arms, thinking to catch anyone trying to escape, but Odysseus was much craftier than to try this.

Later that night, Odysseus stole branches from the monster's bed, and with them, he yoked the sheep together three abreast. Then he quietly ordered his surviving companions to cling to the fleecy belly of each middle ram. Odysseus himself chose the biggest and sturdiest ram of all, yoking it to no other sheep, but clinging to its belly alone.

They spent the rest of the night hanging upside down beneath the sheep. When rosy-fingered Dawn appeared, Polyphemus let his flocks out to pasture. As the sheep trotted out of the cave, the Cyclops groped the top of each sheep to make sure no one was riding out of the cave to freedom. Odysseus's ram was last of all. As it approached the mouth of the cave, Polyphemus stopped it.

"Old ram, why are you last to leave? You're always first. You're biggest and strongest of all! Perhaps you're hanging back in sympathy for your master's having been blinded by a horrible man and his companions after they got me drunk! But this Nobody isn't out of the woods just yet. Old ram, if only you could speak, surely you'd tell me where he is hiding."

Odysseus shivered as Polyphemus patted the ram's back before it waddled out into the sunshine. Once at a distance from the cave, he and his men let go of the sheep's bellies and scrambled back down the mountain, hauling with them as many lambs as they could carry. When he finally reached the safety of his ship, Odysseus couldn't contain himself: "You!" he hollered up toward the Cyclops. "You who dared eat your own guests! I hope you're enjoying Zeus's punishment!"

Polyphemus, though blind, was not deaf. He hurled a jagged chunk of the mountain toward the voice below. It grazed Odysseus's ship as it tumbled into the sea, and the resulting wave was so great that it washed the vessel onto the shore. Odysseus's men pushed the ship offshore and rowed fast out of danger. Twice as far from land as before, Odysseus made as if to call again to the great beast, but his crew begged him to refrain and to be thankful for one lucky escape.

"Cyclops!" cried stubborn Odysseus, "If anyone asks you why you are sightless, you can tell him you were blinded by Odysseus of Ithaca, son of Laertes, sacker of cities!"

Polyphemus realized an old prophecy had come to fruition and prayed to Poseidon not to let Odysseus make it home—but if he did, he would lose all his companions and find trouble on his arrival. Polyphemus hurled another massive peak into the ocean that just missed the ship, but again the resulting wave thrust Odysseus's ship upon the shore. This time, however, it landed in a spot farther along the coast, where the rest of his fleet waited. Together, the crews feasted upon the fat flocks of the Cyclops and drank sweet wine late into the night. When Dawn's rosy glow spread across the sky, they dashed their oars into the gray sea and sailed on, glad to have escaped death but grieving for the loss of their companions.

But they were merely on to their next adventure. For Poseidon, having heard the Cyclops's prayer, churned the seas in anger and caused many storms for Odysseus before the hero reached home.

THE BIRTH OF ATHENA

Zeus's first wife was Metis, whose name means Cunning Wisdom. She was a nymph, the daughter of Oceanus and Tethys.

After they were married, Metis was uninterested in making love. Capable of turning herself into any form she pleased, she evaded Zeus's grasp by assuming one shape after another. Zeus continued in his pursuit, however, and eventually he succeeded in making Metis pregnant. But Zeus's parents, Gaia (Earth) and Uranus (Sky), told him Metis was destined to bear a powerful son who would replace his father as king of the gods.

Zeus schemed ways to avoid the prophecy and concluded that the best solution was to get rid of Metis altogether. One day, he sweet-talked her, and when she wasn't paying attention, he swallowed her whole. Now, Zeus possessed not just physical strength—Cunning Wisdom was inside him, too.

Metis, of course, was pregnant, so when Zeus devoured her, he also swallowed his offspring. Before long, his head swelled up like a balloon, and he developed an unbearable headache. The blacksmith god Hephaestus (though some say it was wily Prometheus) hit Zeus's head with a bronze axe, and out of his head sprang Athena, goddess of war and wisdom, fully clothed and armed. She yelped a war cry to announce her arrival, and Sky and Earth both shivered, causing golden snowflakes to fall to Earth.

Pale-eyed Athena was renowned for her wisdom; after all, she'd been born from the seat of knowledge—her father's head. Daughter of strength and *metis*, Athena became the patron goddess of Athens.

HERMES AND
THE CATTLE OF APOLLO

Hermes, son of Zeus and the nymph Maia, was born one morning in his mother's cave on Mount Cyllene. Swaddled in his cradle, he grew restless, so he got up to go for a walk.

He came across a tortoise, and, admiring its mottled shell, he brought it home, where he scooped the poor creature out, stretched cowhide across the underside of the shell, and added seven sheepgut strings. With his new instrument, the lyre, he sang melodiously of his parents and of his birth.

As noontime approached, he grew hungry. Not for mother's milk, like a normal baby, though. Hermes had a hankering for meat, and his desire necessitated a thievish plan.

That evening, he set off for the mountain meadows where Apollo tended his cattle. He quickly rounded up fifty lowing crumple-horned cows and, making them walk backwards, herded them all the way to Pylos, where he hid them in a cave. Then he gathered laurel branches and invented fire. He sacrificed two cows, cutting up the meat and roasting it, and made twelve portions, to give each of the gods a share. Afterward he stretched the hides on the rocks.

The smell of roasting meat made Hermes' mouth water. Oh, for a taste! But he resisted, knowing that poaching cattle was one thing; eating them was another. He hid the traces of his theft and sacrifice, threw ash over the embers, and at daybreak returned to his mother's cave, where he crept back to his cradle, careful not to make a sound.

Maia knew—as mothers always somehow do—that he'd been sneaking around, and she scolded him for being a pest, warning him that, sooner or later, Apollo would discover the theft of his cattle and come looking for him. Hermes, all charm, replied, "Look at me! I'm just a newborn babe! How can you accuse me of such trickery?"

Maia was right. Apollo soon noticed that some of his herd had gone missing, but, he found that, oddly, the tracks led right back to the pasture. He interrogated everyone in the vicinity until an old man admitted he'd seen a small boy herding cows. Apollo immediately marched up to Maia's cave.

"What have you done with my cattle, Hermes?" he demanded. "Tell me now, or I'll throw you into the darkest corner of the Underworld!"

"My main concerns—being a baby," cooed Hermes in reply, "are sleep, warm baths, and mother's milk. After all," he added, eyes twinkling, "I was only born yesterday."

Apollo was no fool. "Boy!" he shouted, "I wasn't born yesterday!" And he whisked baby Hermes off to visit justice-bringing Zeus. On the way to Mount Olympus, Hermes belched loudly and sneezed, surprising Apollo, who dropped him in disgust. He contemplated the boy for a moment, but scooped him up again. Soon, they found themselves before Zeus.

Apollo repeated his accusations and Hermes again denied them. Zeus laughed at his devilish son, but, suspecting lies, he asked Hermes to lead the way to the stolen cows. Hermes obliged, and when they arrived at the herd, Apollo was content—until something caught his eye.

Drying on a sun-warmed rock were two cowhides.

Furious, Apollo cut willow branches and bound Hermes, but the switches only fell off his body and grew into trees. While Apollo plotted a suitable punishment, Hermes played a tune on his lyre to amuse himself. As he paced, Apollo heard the notes carried across the wind and, entranced, asked to play. What sweet song Apollo made with that tortoiseshell! Fifty cows suddenly seemed a small price to pay for a lyre . . .

Such was the start of Hermes, messenger and trickster, patron of thieves, guide of souls.

DESIRE

THE MINOTAUR

When Minos became king of Crete, he boasted that the gods themselves had willed it and that as proof Poseidon would make a bull rise from the sea. Sure enough, the ocean yielded a bull so handsome, so soft, so extraordinarily gentle, that Minos could not bear to sacrifice the animal to Poseidon, as he had agreed. Thinking the god of the sea probably wouldn't know the difference, Minos slaughtered a different bull in its place. But omniscient Poseidon did notice and was so incensed that in revenge he struck Minos's wife Pasiphae with desire.

Not just any desire—she desired the bull.

Pasiphae's yearning was insatiable. Every day, she gazed out at the bull in its pasture and dreamed of becoming its mistress. She soon enlisted the help of the inventor and craftsman Daedalus, who built her a hollow wooden cow with wheels. When Pasiphae climbed into the cow, Daedalus rolled it out into the meadow, and as the bull drew near, Pasiphae's breath quickened, she pulled up her robes and bent over. At last, her desire was fulfilled.

From this union, Pasiphae bore a half-man, half-bovine creature called the Minotaur. Minos ordered Daedalus to imprison it, so the inventor built the Labyrinth, a sprawling maze coiled with twisting paths, so confusing that he could hardly find his way out once he'd finished.

To feed the Minotaur, which lived on human flesh, Minos ordered the Athenians to send youths to Crete to be thrown in the Labyrinth and eaten before they could escape.

After many years, a young man named Theseus, believing he could kill the beast, volunteered to be sent to Crete. Why not? He had, after all, already killed the bull at Marathon.

When Theseus arrived at Minos's palace, Ariadne, daughter of Minos and Pasiphae, fell in love with him. After consulting Daedalus about how to escape the Labyrinth, Ariadne offered assistance to Theseus if he would take her back to Athens and marry her. He assented, and with Ariadne's instructions and a ball of thread, Theseus entered the Labyrinth, tying one end of the thread to the doorpost behind him and letting the ball unravel in his hand as he walked. When Theseus discovered the Minotaur, he killed it with his bare hands, and then he rewound the thread, triumphantly making his way back to the entrance.

Taking along young Ariadne, he quickly left the island, and after a night's sail put in just off the island of Naxos for a rest. While Theseus explored the island, Ariadne took a nap on the beach.

When she awoke, she saw the hull of his black-sailed ship fast distancing itself from Naxos. Theseus had never loved her, she realized—he'd only needed her help. Standing there on the beach, alone, Ariadne wept with anger and regret. She resolved to climb to the top of the cliffs to throw herself into the sea, but as she ascended, she heard strange things—laughter, drunken singing, hoofsteps.

For Dionysus had seen Ariadne there on the beach, her eyes glittering with tears, and found her pitiful and lovely. He descended to Naxos, and marrying her, made her immortal, later setting her crown in the starry sky to twinkle forever.

HELEN AND PARIS

The wedding of Peleus and Thetis was a lavish affair, with all the gods in attendance. All, that is, except Eris (Strife), for who wants trouble at a wedding?

When Eris discovered she hadn't been asked to attend, she invited herself. She arrived just after Peleus and Thetis retired to the bridal chamber, and the festivities were in full swing—guests were singing and dancing and drinking nectar and wine—so her presence went unnoticed. Into the crowd she tossed an apple, a single, innocent apple. The symbol of love. A golden fruit from the gardens of the Hesperides. A *kallisteion*, as Eris put it—a beautyprize.

The guests parted in surprise as the gleaming fruit bounced and tumbled amongst them. It came to a standstill at the feet of three goddesses huddled together chatting, where its inscription twinkled in the lamplight: "For the fair."

Hera, Aphrodite, and Athena all reached for it at once.

Three self-certain claims. A single golden apple. None would acquiesce. It was time for Zeus to intervene.

Zeus, however, found himself unable to settle the matter. Hera was his wife, but Athena was his daughter, and if he chose Aphrodite, everyone would accuse him of lust.

So Zeus, as gods are wont to do, passed the task off to someone else. He asked Hermes to take the goddesses to visit Paris, who lived on Mount Ida in Crete. Paris was the son of the king of Troy, but he lived modestly as a shepherd.

The contest for the golden apple went like this: Each goddess showed herself to Paris nude. Overwhelmed by the spectacle of three naked goddesses, Paris asked them to please appear individually. Hera, goddess of marriage, went first, promising Paris that if he chose her, he'd become a great ruler of men. He thanked her and called in Athena. The gray-eyed goddess of war promised that if she were selected, he would become a hero and would always be victorious in battle. He thanked her, ruefully noting that Troy and its usual enemy, Lydia, were currently at peace. Aphrodite went last. Standing nude before Paris, the goddess of love flattered him and complimented his good looks. She even flirted with him a little, though Paris was immune to all that, of course. Then Aphrodite played her trump card: She promised him Helen, the most beautiful woman in all of Greece. And, Aphrodite added, as soon as Helen took a single look at him—despite the fact that she was the wife of Menelaus—she'd fall in love.

There was Paris, asked to choose the fairest goddess, and offered the fairest mortal.

He voted for Aphrodite. Who wouldn't?

Hera and Athena were henceforth enemies of the Trojans.

Aphrodite told Paris to appear at the court of Menelaus in Sparta, and to be patient. On the tenth day of Paris's visit, Menelaus left to attend a funeral, and Helen was left to entertain the guests. When she appeared before them, radiant and charming, Paris wanted to make love to her then and there, in the banquet hall.

It wasn't difficult to seduce her—after all, the goddess of love was on his side—and soon Helen, entranced by her new lover, ran away with Paris.

Although some say Hera caused a storm that blew the couple's ship off course to Phoenicia, and others say she gave Paris a cloud that looked like Helen while Hermes whisked away the real queen of Sparta to Egypt for safekeeping,

I believe the truth to be more mundane; Helen and Paris probably reached Troy in three days with good winds.

When Menelaus returned home and found his wife had disappeared, he set off for Troy with Odysseus to get her back. With Aphrodite on the side of the lovers, however, Menelaus's effort was unsuccessful. He returned to Greece and asked his brother Agamemnon, in Mycenae, to furnish an army and help him wage war.

Thus, immortal vanity and mortal weakness begat the Trojan War. Eris, still smarting, bore Toil, Neglect, Starvation, Pain, Battles, Combats, Bloodshed, Slaughter, Quarrels, Lies, Pretenses, Arguments, Disorder, Disaster, and Oath. It was a mess.

After many years, it was agreed that Paris and Menelaus should have a one-on-one battle, the winner of which would take Helen as his wife and call a truce. But just as the two men were about to settle things, Aphrodite plucked Paris from the battlefield and deposited him in his bedroom. Then she went to retrieve Helen, who resisted—she'd gotten a bit tired of Paris, to be honest, but Aphrodite countered: If Helen didn't comply, she would incur the goddess's wrath. Helen sullenly retired to the bedchamber, where Paris waited. While they made love, Menelaus searched the battlefield—here was the moment to defeat Paris, but the devil had disappeared.

When, later, Paris was killed, the king of Troy offered Helen as a prize to the bravest. Helen was disgusted; she'd really had enough of the city and was ready to go home. Her lover was dead, her husband was here to rescue her—the war couldn't be over soon enough. So when she bumped into Odysseus, who had infiltrated the city disguised as a beggar, she didn't betray him but instead helped him capture Troy.

On the night they'd agreed upon to escape, Helen waited for Menelaus. When the king of Sparta saw his wife, however, after all those years of battle, he wasn't in

much of a mood for reconciliation, so rather than embracing her, Menelaus drew his sword and charged. Helen fixed her gaze upon him, looked him straight in the eye, and then, slowly she dropped her robe to reveal one perfect breast. Menelaus halted and put down his sword, and, overcome with desire, fell at her feet.

Menelaus took Helen back to Greece on his swift ship, but when they landed, the Greeks welcomed Helen with fury. Having been at war for her sake for ten years, they wanted to stone her to death.

So there was Helen disembarking the ship, faced by Greeks with stones in their hands. What then?

Desire, beholden to no one, overtook them. They dropped their stones in awe and longing.

Helen walked home.

PYGMALION

When the women of Cyprus refused to worship Aphrodite, the goddess turned them into prostitutes. After that, the king of Cyprus, Pygmalion, gave up looking for a wife and turned himself toward other pursuits.

For a king, he was a talented sculptor, and he went to work on a female figure, carving it from ivory the color of freshly fallen snow. When he finished, he had created a woman whose beauty surpassed that of any mortal.

Pygmalion often caressed the sculpture, running his fingers over the curves he'd so delicately worked. How quickly one's hand slid across the surface, he thought. He squeezed her waist, certain his fingers sank into flesh, being careful not to bruise her. He gave his statue gifts—seashells, polished gems, parakeets in cages, lilies, amber. He draped her in sensual fabrics, placed gems upon her fingers and chains around her neck, adorned her with earrings and ribbons. He preferred her naked and pure, though, and he even made her a bed of down. How chaste she was, he thought, how unlike the women of Cyprus! It was as if she could move, but only modesty held her back.

When the feast day of Aphrodite arrived, Pygmalion dutifully sacrificed in her honor and prayed. Unable to bring himself to ask for what he really wanted, Pygmalion whispered to the goddess, "I'd like a wife *like* the statue."

He went home to his ivory companion and couldn't resist a quick kiss. He breathed upon the cool ivory curve of her neck, and when he pressed his lips against hers, he was sure he felt warmth. He pressed himself against her thigh, certain it

yielded just a bit. Or was he going mad? Let me do it once more, he thought. Just a nibble on the ear—I'm sure the texture is softer than before. Just a kiss on the cheek—I'm sure the color is rosier than before. Pygmalion lost himself in desire. And then, two dark eyes looked up at him.

How could stone ever be transformed to flesh? Was it the sheer weight of longing? Was it persistence? Was it the folly of believing so completely?

Does it matter? Aphrodite attended the wedding.

VANITY

ICARUS

Daedalus surpassed all others in invention: He designed a fortress, built a gold honeycomb for Aphrodite, invented masts and sailyards, and even created a portable folding chair. He also excelled as a sculptor: His statues possessed open eyes and free-moving arms and hands, and they were so lifelike, it was said that only the Ethiopians surpassed him in skill, for their statues could also speak. Daedalus was so talented, it was rumored he'd been blessed by Athena herself.

Despite his talent, or perhaps because of it, people said that he was jealous of his nephew, who apprenticed for him. When the young man died, Daedalus was accused of murder and exiled. He found solace at the palace of King Minos on Crete, where he quickly settled into the perfect niche: Creator of Wooden Images.

When Ariadne asked Daedalus how Theseus could escape from the Labyrinth, he told her—after all, he had designed the maze. But when Minos found out the inventor played a part in Theseus's escape, he decided to exile Daedalus and his son, Icarus. On second thought, he mused, Daedalus would only find a way to achieve a comfortable life again. What more perfect punishment, thought Minos, than for Daedalus to die at the hands of one of his own inventions?

Once imprisoned, Daedalus and his son soon discovered it was futile to try to find their way out of the Labyrinth: The trick with the string only worked if you started from the entrance. Daedalus prayed to the heavens above and, indeed, from the sky came his inspiration. His supplies were meager, but he built frames out of twine and carefully attached feathers with wax.

Before they took flight, Daedalus instructed Icarus to watch the skies, stay especially far from the constellations Bootes and Orion, and follow his father as guide. "Chart a middle path," he cautioned the boy. "Don't fly too close to the sun, or the wax will heat up; don't go too close to the sea, or the sea spray will unstick the feathers." Daedalus mounted the wings on Icarus's and then his own shoulders and embraced his son.

The feathered structures worked, carrying father and son out of the Labyrinth, above the palace, and high into the sky. Daedalus looked back every so often at Icarus, who beamed back, delighted with flight. As they flew away from the island, Icarus laughed and whooped and flapped his wings. Fishermen stopped casting their lines, shepherds ceased watching their sheep, farmers halted plowing their fields—all to wonder at the flight of the inventor and his son. The pair flew over Samos, sacred to Hera, and Naxos and Delos. They soared past lakes, past groves, past islands rich with honey-making bees.

Icarus flew well, and his fearlessness grew. He began to think he was quite good at flying. What was this business about a middle path? What did his father know, anyway? His father spent his time constructing things, like a giant bovine sex toy to satisfy a perverted queen and an absurd, life-size hedgerow puzzlepark in which men had perished at the horns of a half-bull beast to amuse a sadistic king. *Honestly,* what did his father know? Chart the middle path! Why settle for mediocrity when he, Icarus, could soar?

The birds in the sky marveled at him. He flew higher and higher, so high that the wax binding together the wings softened. But Icarus didn't descend; enchanted by his ability to fly, he didn't even notice anything was wrong. Suddenly, the wax succumbed to the heat of the sun and dripped down through the sky, hitting the ocean like hail. Icarus flapped wings no longer; he flapped only arms.

There was Icarus, treading the wind as if it was water, looking downward at the sea. As he plummeted seaward, he screamed to his father for help, but Daedalus, far ahead on his middle path, heard nothing.

As Daedalus turned to check on his son, a splash drew his glance downward. Feathers floated upon the gray-blue sea.

ECHO AND NARCISSUS

Echo was a nymph who hunted in Artemis's band. While riding through the forest, she spotted a young man on horseback, tall and tanned, soft ringlets framing his jaw. Echo dismounted and hid herself behind a tree to admire the stranger, and as the barking of her mistress's hounds grew fainter, she crept toward the boy, who, not noticing her, rode away. Never letting him out of her sight, Echo scampered after him as he continued deep into the forest. All day she followed him (her own horse forgotten), and when night fell and the boy lay down on a bed of moss and leaves, Echo rested, too, and dreamed of him.

Day after day, she followed the boy, never saying a word, blending in among the trees and making herself as thin as the fluttering reeds. But he, Narcissus, never once noticed his extra shadow, for he was oblivious to anyone but himself. Though he stirred desire in men and women alike, he scorned the concept of love.

Echo's infatuation increased by the day, but though she yearned for Narcissus, she couldn't even say his name. This wasn't shyness, however: Years before, Echo had distracted Hera with long stories so Zeus could frolic with other nymphs. When Hera discovered the deceitful purpose of Echo's chattering, she condemned Echo to never be able to speak first and to always have to repeat what others said.

Echo continued her silent pursuit of Narcissus until one day Narcissus became separated from his hunting companions and called out to find them.

"Who's here?" Narcissus hollered into the forest.

"Here!" Echo shouted back enthusiastically.

"Then come!" said Narcissus.

Echo couldn't believe it. "Come!" she shouted.

Narcissus believed his companions were making fun of him. "Why do you shun me?" he asked.

"Why do you shun *me*?" Echo replied.

"Then, let us join!" shouted Narcissus, annoyed.

Echo emphatically agreed. "Let us join!" she cried, leaping out of her hiding place and flinging her arms around him.

Narcissus, disgusted, shoved her aside. As he rode off, Echo cried his last words over and over: "Let us join! Let us join! Let us join!" She sought the darkest corner of the forest and cried for days, neither eating nor sleeping. Slowly, she wasted away, until nothing remained of Echo but her repeating voice.

For Narcissus, nothing changed. Observing the desperation of his admirers, he steeled himself against love. Years later, after a long day of hunting, he dismounted at a pool in the forest. There was no breeze, and the water was still and clear, its surface unmarred by floating twigs or leaves. As he knelt down to drink, he met his reflection. Narcissus stared at the young man, who returned his steady gaze. "What's your name?" he asked, but he couldn't hear the reply. He reached out to caress the boy, but as his hand slid into the water, the figure only drew farther away. Hours passed, but Narcissus remained, transfixed by the image of the young man. He wept, cursing the gods for the cruelty of such emotion, and as he wept his tears cascaded upon the surface of the water, breaking the reflection into a thousand ripples. "Don't go!" he cried out.

"Let us join, let us join, let us join," whispered the forest.

. . .

Narcissus, captivated by his own gaze, died, diving into himself.

DECEIT

TANTALUS

In the age when gods and men dined together, Tantalus was often invited to feast with the Olympians. To reciprocate the favor, he threw his own banquet and invited the gods.

For the feast, Tantalus slaughtered his son, Pelops, and cut him up and boiled him. No one knows exactly why he did this. Most likely, Tantalus wished to test the omniscience of the gods, though he may have been trying to outdo them in their hospitality by serving the rarest delicacy.

When they sat down to dine, the gods did notice that it was human flesh they'd been served and were horrified. Only grief-filled Demeter absentmindedly ate any of the dish—a piece of Pelops's shoulder. Hermes put all of the pieces of Pelops back into the pot, and when Pelops emerged alive, with an ivory shoulder to replace the missing chunk, Poseidon immediately fell in love.

Though it was his most despicable crime, this was not Tantalus's only one. During their meals together, the gods confided certain things to Tantalus. Unfortunately, Tantalus, who had a penchant for gossip, tattled the mysteries of the gods to his fellow mortals. In addition to trusting him with secrets, the gods fed Tantalus nectar and ambrosia, which made him immortal. Tantalus stole this food of the gods for his mates so that they could become immortal, too.

It took Zeus but little time to concoct a suitable punishment for Tantalus: He cast him into the Underworld and condemned him to eternal hunger and thirst. Tantalus stood in a lake that rose up to his chin, but whenever he tried to take a

drink, the water immediately receded. Likewise, fruit trees grew above him, bearing all sorts of ripe fruits—apples, figs, pears, pomegranates, olives. Though the branches grew all the way down to his shoulders, whenever he tried to pluck a fruit, wind lifted the branches high above his head.

From Tantalus comes the word *tantalizing*—tempting, but just out of reach.

PROMETHEUS

There came a time when the gods wished to cease dining with men, perhaps because of troublemakers like Tantalus, so they asked Prometheus (Forethought) to help in the division of food.

Prometheus was a crafty fellow—it was he who created men from water and earth. To determine how the goods should be divided between the gods (represented by Zeus) and men, he sacrificed a cow. He carefully sliced off the juicy bits of meat from the bones and placed them inside the slimy stomach of the cow. Then he wrapped up the bones in the glistening, rich fat—which everyone knows is the tastiest part. He placed the stomach in front of the men and the fat in front of Zeus.

"Prometheus," said Zeus, "this cow appears unfairly split."

"Well," Prometheus began, barely able to restrain a smile, "fair or not, take whichever you want. Why not take the best bits? Why let men have them?"

Zeus chose the rich package of fat. He probably knew Prometheus was up to no good. Maybe he even chose the fatty package on purpose, just to get Prometheus in trouble. Or perhaps Prometheus really did outwit Zeus. No one knows for sure.

When Zeus unwrapped his bundle, he found that the glistening outside layer hid a pile of white bones thoroughly stripped of meat. How could men get meat but the gods get bones? This wasn't justice—it was trickery! But he had chosen, so nothing could be done. This is why when men sacrifice animals, they burn the bones

on altars for the smoke to rise up to the gods, while they themselves get to eat roasted meat.

Although Zeus couldn't change the outcome, he could get revenge by withholding fire from men. Men might have meat, but without fire, they couldn't cook it, and that meant they'd have nothing to eat.

Under Zeus's wrath, men faced extinction. Prometheus, concerned, paid a visit to Zeus on Mount Olympus, taking a giant stalk of fennel as his walking stick. While he was on Olympus, he stole seeds of fire and hid them inside the hollow stalk. The embers smoldered as Prometheus descended to Earth.

When deep-thundering Zeus saw flames on Earth, he knew there was only one way men could have gotten fire: Prometheus. Zeus couldn't allow himself to be outcrafted. Prometheus's antics were getting embarrassing, and he deserved punishment once and for all.

Zeus ordered Kratos (Power) and Bia (Force) to bring Prometheus to the Caucasus Mountains in Scythia, where Hephaestus bound him to the rocks. At daybreak, an eagle perched on Prometheus and pecked at his abdomen, digging down through his skin to feast on his liver. The torture ended at sunset, but Prometheus miraculously healed during the night. The next morning, though, the eagle feasted again. And so it continued, day after day.

Zeus wasn't finished; he still wanted to punish men. "Men with their roasted meat!" he bellowed. "I'll give them an evil that they'll enjoy while it destroys them!" He ordered Hephaestus to mix water and earth to form a young woman, a *parthenos*, modeled after the immortal goddesses. Hephaestus added strength, Athena adorned her with an embroidered veil and a golden diadem, Persuasion draped golden necklaces upon her, and the Graces bedecked her with garlands of spring flowers. Aphrodite poured grace over her head, and Hermes gave her a voice and named her Pandora (Allgift), for she was a gift from all the gods to men.

Zeus, having had many lovers, knew exactly what men would fall for. But just to be on the safe side, he sent Pandora to the most gullible man of all, Prometheus's brother Epimetheus (Afterthought). Although Prometheus warned his brother never to accept gifts from the gods—Zeus in particular—when Hermes arrived with Pandora, Epimetheus was besotted and forgot his brother's advice. He married her immediately.

So far, you might think that Pandora doesn't sound all that bad—she's attractive and charming, and she'll become the mother of all women. She certainly doesn't seem malevolent. But Zeus was not so transparent. Just as Prometheus hid bones in a delicious package, Zeus concealed Pandora's dark side beneath her seductive exterior. Along with her good looks, Pandora possessed a deceitful, mischievous mind, for, after all, it was Hermes, the trickster, who had given her speech, so with it came cunning lies and crafty words. And along with grace, Aphrodite had poured yearning and limb-gnawing sorrow over her head.

Until then, men had lived in a pretty pleasant state of affairs. Though now they had to work for their food, they lived without any considerable evils. There was no sickness, hard toil, disease, or torment. Until, that is, Pandora got ahold of that famous jar.

It was in fact a jar, not a box. No one knows exactly who she got it from, though Zeus is a prime suspect. No one knows why she opened it, either. Did she know what it contained and open it out of malice? Or was it simple curiosity that got the better of her? Whatever her motivation, when Pandora raised the lid, every evil now known to humankind swooped out of the jar, and when she lowered it, she trapped Hope inside. Others say it was all the good things that escaped, returning to the heavens and leaving humans alone with hardships.

However evils came to dwell with humans, Zeus delivered them in an irresistible package.

VENGEANCE

MEDEA

The day a youth named Jason arrived at the court of King Aeëtes of Colchis (a kingdom east of the Black Sea) didn't seem much different from any other day. When he received an audience with the king, Jason explained at length how he and the crew of the *Argo*, the Argonauts, were on a mission to retrieve the Golden Fleece. They had been sent by King Pelias in Iolcus, for Pelias, fearing Jason's claim to the throne, charged him with an impossible errand. Aeëtes found this tale so long-winded and bizarre that rather than feeling sympathy for Jason, he suspected the young man of trying to rob him and steal *his* throne. So he told Jason he could have the Golden Fleece if he could yoke two fierce bulls and sow dragons' teeth, knowing that every other man who'd attempted these tasks had died trying.

Aeëtes' daughter, Medea, was only moderately interested in Jason's mission— that is, until that sly pest of a god Eros shot her with one of his famous arrows, inflaming her with desire. She was not so smitten, however, as to believe Jason could perform feats that no one had ever accomplished before. She approached Jason with a deal: She'd provide all the secrets necessary to retrieve the Golden Fleece if he would marry her and take her to Greece.

Jason agreed, and Medea gave him a fire-resistant ointment of drugs and olive oil and outlined how to proceed. Following her directions carefully, he sacrificed a sheep and rubbed himself with the ointment. He then approached the two bronze-hoofed, fire-breathing bulls and successfully yoked them. Next, Jason sacrificed

another sheep, ploughed a field, and sowed the dragon teeth, and when warriors grew from the soil, he fought them and won.

Aeëtes was unpleasantly surprised to find Jason triumphantly returned, but he described where Jason could find the Golden Fleece. Jason soon discovered that laying his hands on it wouldn't be so easy: A massive serpent, as big as a fifty-oared ship, guarded the Fleece. Luckily, Medea intervened again, lulling the great beast to sleep, and Jason claimed his prize.

Medea knew her father was biding his time before killing Jason and the Argonauts, so she helped them cast off in the dark of night. Aeëtes awoke to discover that not only the Argonauts but also his son and daughter had escaped quietly—with the Golden Fleece. He set forth in furious pursuit.

The Argonauts needed to slow Aeëtes' pace, and Medea knew one certain way: She killed her younger brother, cut him up, and threw the pieces overboard. Sure enough, her father and his crew slowed down to pick up the body parts out of the sea and lost the trail of the *Argo*.

When the Argonauts arrived in Iolcus, they discovered that Pelias, believing Jason dead, had killed Jason's mother, father, and younger brother in case they wanted revenge. Jason and Medea immediately made their way to the palace, but they didn't reveal any of their displeasure. Instead, Medea took the king's daughters aside and explained that she knew magic and could make their father young again. They were suspicious, but Medea cut a ram into pieces, and boiled it with herbs in a giant pot, and after a short while she pulled out a live lamb. Convinced of the procedure's efficacy, Pelias's daughters killed him and cut him into pieces, but when they finished boiling him, they found only a mess of soggy flesh. Medea shrugged—they must not have added enough herbs, she said.

Jason and Medea fled to Corinth, where they made a home, had two sons, and lived together as a model of happiness and harmony—until one day, Jason up and left.

Medea was shocked. He'd left her for a younger woman, the daughter of the king of Corinth. Medea envisioned herself divorced and alone, left with nothing. She thought she'd rather die than suffer such humiliation. She'd given up her home and her family for her husband. And she'd done so much for him—made magical potions, chanted incantations. She'd boiled a king! She'd even killed her own brother! How much more devoted could a wife be?

Medea cursed everything and everyone around her. When the king of Corinth heard of her fury, he ordered her into exile, but Medea paid him a visit and persuaded him to let her stay in Corinth for one more day to get her affairs in order. After all, she argued, how much could go wrong in a single day?

Next, Medea confronted Jason, who countered that the marriage had been the king's idea and that no one could refuse the king.

"And besides," he noted, "isn't marrying into the royal family the best thing I could do for our sons?"

"On top of everything, you want my sons? What would be left for me?" Medea snapped and stormed out.

After a few hours, she returned. "You're right, you're right," she said hoarsely, wiping fat tears from her cheeks. "I was wrong. Please take our sons. Raise them as royalty. I'll send them over to meet their new stepmother."

Jason agreed to take them in.

You didn't really think Medea had changed her mind, did you? The boys gave their stepmother two gifts, a robe and a golden diadem, both laced with poison. They burst into flame the minute the girl tried them on.

Although Medea had now prevented Jason from remarrying, she hadn't exorcised her fury. When the children returned from their errand they found their mother weeping, a knife in her hand. What million thoughts must have raced through her mind? Did she hesitate as she pulled each son's head back by his hair? Did she avert her eyes as she slit their throats?

Medea fled Corinth victoriously in a chariot driven by serpents, given to her by her grandfather, Helios.

And Jason? In truth, he never recovered. The famous hero who captured the Golden Fleece would often sit beneath his illustrious *Argo,* cursing his fate or musing on times past. One day, a chunk of rotting prow toppled off and killed him.

Medea, on the other hand, remarried and lived happily in Athens for many years.

GRIEF

DEMETER AND PERSEPHONE

Zeus promised his daughter Persephone to his brother Hades, king of the Underworld, but he didn't ask Persephone's mother, Demeter, what she thought of the match. He certainly didn't try to persuade Persephone herself, for who wants to be queen of the Underworld?

Persephone was young, chaste, a perfect *parthenos*, unconcerned about men or sex or marriage. She often spent her afternoons with her girlfriends in the meadows picking flowers—lilies, irises, roses, crocuses, violets, hyacinths. So, to capture Persephone, Zeus asked Gaia (Earth) to grow a flower of exceptional beauty—a narcissus, no less—in Persephone's favorite meadow.

The narcissus had a hundred voluptuous blossoms and possessed an exquisite perfume. Persephone was naturally drawn to it, though she didn't mention the flower to her friends: This one she wanted all for herself. As she reached down greedily with both hands to pluck it, the earth began to thunder from inside. She drew back, but then the ground itself opened up before her. From the gaping chasm came galloping horses pulling Hades in his terrifying chariot, and he snatched her by the waist and wheeled off. Persephone cried for help, her hair flying, strewing a trail of flowers behind her.

Persephone screamed as Hades spurred his horses on and his chariot plummeted downward. Her screams echoed between mountaintops, sifted down through the sea, sank to the bottom of underground lakes and sulfurous springs. But no one heard her—or so it seemed: Actually, Helios (the Sun), who can see everything from above, heard her, and Hecate did too, but neither came to her rescue.

Some say that as Hades descended, a nymph tried to stop him, telling him that no matter how desirous one might be, it was always better to woo with honeyed words and to obtain a mother's blessing than to abduct a girl, but Hades vengefully dissolved the nymph into water.

When Persephone didn't return home that evening, Demeter grew worried. For nine days and nine nights she searched for Persephone by torchlight, not even eating or drinking, grieving for the loss of her only daughter. No one could tell her what had happened to Persephone. On Demeter's tenth day of wandering, Hecate confessed she'd heard Persephone's screams but hadn't seen the abductor. Then Helios revealed that Hades had carried her off. "It was Zeus's doing," he justified. "But as husbands go, Hades isn't a bad choice. He is, after all, lord of the Underworld."

Demeter was furious with Helios and Hecate and all the other gods for conspiring against her. Most of all, she was disgusted with Zeus, so much so that she left Mount Olympus to go live among men. She adopted the form of a mortal and went to Eleusis, where she sat upon a rock for so long, and so miserably, that the rock came to be called "Unlaughing," after her. She often cursed Gaia for having helped Zeus and Hades abduct her daughter, so though she was the goddess of grain and fertile harvests, Demeter spitefully let all the crops on Earth wither. Soon, famine threatened to consume all mortals.

Every Olympian came to Demeter, bearing gifts to persuade her to return to Olympus and to restore the harvest, but none succeeded. It seemed Demeter might grieve forever. Zeus had no choice but to send Hermes down to the Underworld to convince Hades to return Persephone.

Cunning Hermes won Hades over, but before Hades sent the girl back, he gave her a pomegranate seed. And Persephone, perhaps distracted by the excitement of returning home, swallowed it.

That single seed sealed Persephone's fate. For everyone knows that the living may leave the Underworld as long as they do not eat anything there. Now Persephone could live with her mother only two-thirds of the year; the other third, the dark months of winter, she would be required to return to the Underworld.

. . .

Persephone returns to Earth every spring when her favorite flowers blossom and departs long after the harvest, after the leaves have fallen from the trees and the days have grown cold. And every year, while crops lie dormant underground and her daughter reigns below, Demeter still grieves.

AJAX AND THE CONTEST OF ARMS

When Achilles was a baby, his mother, Thetis, dipped him in the river Styx to make him immortal. But his heel, by which she'd dangled him in the water, remained dry and was therefore his only vulnerable spot. As was Achilles' fate, his heel was wounded by Paris during the Trojan War. You'd think only a god could direct such a perfect shot—indeed, Apollo guided Paris's arrow.

When Ajax came back from battle lugging Achilles' corpse, the Achaeans were devastated, for Achilles had been the greatest warrior of them all. They wailed in mourning and held lavish funeral games in his honor, complete with foot races, archery contests, chariot races, and more. Ajax won the discus throw.

To bequeath Achilles' armor and weapons to the second-greatest Achaean warrior, a debate was held. It featured only two contestants: Ajax and Odysseus. Ajax went first, reminding his companions of his glorious lineage.

"Friends, don't think me boastful, but let me remind you that not only am I Zeus's great-grandson, I am Achilles' cousin. It should really be a family member who inherits Achilles' arms. And also, don't you remember how Odysseus actually tried to shirk coming to Troy to join you by pretending to be crazy? How could you award arms to a man who never wanted to bear them in the first place? Besides, why would Odysseus need new arms? His aren't even scratched! They've practically never seen battle!"

The crowd laughed, and Ajax finished, "But I saved the Greek ships from Hector's fire. I saved Agamemnon's life. I battled fearsome Hector. Odysseus? He's not a brave soldier. He's just a rascal who uses tricks and traps to succeed!"

Ajax strode back to the crowd, and Odysseus took the stand, wiping his eyes as if he'd been weeping.

"My fellow men," he began, "it's true that Ajax, with his familial ties, lays the stronger claim to arms than I. But I beg you to consider this: It was I who ferreted out our great hero when he was disguised as a girl. And knowing Achilles was crucial to our victory, I brought him to Troy. Who better to receive the arms of Achilles than the man who recruited him? Though my own arms might not be battered from combat, I have certainly sacrificed: I was wounded in battle, something Ajax cannot claim. Let me also remind you that although Ajax fought Hector, he didn't kill him. Finally, remember this: It was I who braved the walls of Troy to steal the Palladium, the statue of Athena we all know is required to capture Troy. Victory will be ours!"

The crowd cheered as Odysseus concluded, "Dear fellows, remember that it is not always sheer force in battle that counts. It is also *metis*, cleverness, that enables success."

The army voted for Odysseus, thus proving his point that true strength is in the mind, not the body. Betrayed by his fellow Achaeans and one-upped by a trickster, Ajax despaired. First was the loss of his best friend, Achilles, and now, this humiliating defeat. Grief stretched limitlessly before him.

That night, after darkness shrouded the camp, Ajax crept toward one of the tents, rope and sword in hand. As he approached the entrance, Athena discovered him and addled his brain to steer him toward the camp's livestock instead. Believing the animals to be his comrades, he bound them together—sheep, bulls, and shepherd dogs—and took them captive inside his tent. He unsheathed his sword and thrust the blade in every direction, stabbing, decapitating, and gouging, sometimes dropping his sword to break necks or spines—so immense was the wrath of Ajax.

The next morning, Athena met him in the camp, and Ajax bragged to her of his revenge. As she led him back to his tent, the stench of slaughtered beasts surrounded him and lifted his madness. When he saw what he had done during the night, Ajax uttered a deep and melancholy sound. "Ai, ai!" he groaned, words that mean "Alas!" but are also the sound of his own name (Aias, in Greek).

Ajax retreated to his tent, where he refused to eat or drink, sitting in shame, caked in blood, and staring into the distance. When finally he emerged from his tent, he wandered far from the camp. Beneath a solitary palm tree, he planted his sword in the earth, aiming it toward the heavens, and as the early glow of Dawn appeared, the sword of Ajax that had felled so many in battle killed the hero himself.

ORPHEUS AND EURYDICE

Orpheus was renowned for his melodic voice and his lyre playing—it was said he could charm animals and even trees in the forest with his music. Soon after he married Eurydice, Aristaeus, son of Apollo, tried to abduct her. As Eurydice ran through the grass to escape Aristaeus, she stepped on a snake and immediately died from the bite. Orpheus, heartbroken by his young wife's death, did the only thing he could—he sang.

His laments for Eurydice could be heard everywhere; the wind carried his notes, and the birds repeated them. The sound of Orpheus's mourning entered every crevice of the earth and filled the sea with longing. He wandered, singing, to Taenarum, where the guard dog Cerberus greeted him, tail wagging, at the gates to the Underworld. As Orpheus descended, all the grief in his heart poured forth, and he confessed he would rather join Eurydice in Hell than return to Earth alone.

As Orpheus sang, the winds of Hell stopped blowing, and the Shades grew tearful. Tantalus stopped trying to drink the water that eternally receded beneath him. The burning wheel to which Ixion was fixed stopped turning. Vultures ceased feasting upon Tityus's liver. The daughters of Danaus stopped filling their leaking bowls destined never to be full. Sisyphus took a rest from rolling his boulder up the mountain. Even the snake-haired Erinyes, those fearful winged creatures in the deepest pit of Hell who whip the dead to madness—even they wept at Orpheus's song.

When he reached Hades and Persephone, Orpheus sang words of flattery and of how love had joined him with Eurydice just as it had joined Hades with Persephone. Though everyone knows this to be a lie—Hades clearly kidnapped the poor girl—it worked and Hades agreed to give Eurydice back. There was a condition, of course: Orpheus must not look at his wife until they reached the world above.

To lead Eurydice, still limping from snakebite, he took her hand. It was warm and soft and smooth, and every so often he'd give it a squeeze, delighted and relieved to have his beloved back. As they walked, though, Orpheus began to wonder: How could he be sure he held Eurydice's hand? Could he be mistaking her for someone else? Or what if she were a ghost? Worse, what if she had been gone so long, he'd forgotten how she felt and what she looked like? The more he tried to concentrate on the ascent, the more he grew desperate to know if it was his wife's hand he held. He shook himself, knowing Hades' condition, and told himself his mind was playing tricks on him. No god could be so cruel as to give him another's hand.

At the edge of the Underworld, a shaft of sunlight broke through the shadows, and he could no longer resist. But as he turned his head, he felt his wife's small hand slip from his grasp.

She was gone.

MADNESS

PENTHEUS

After years of traveling in the East, in lands of leopards and sand, Dionysus returned to his birthplace, Thebes. He sauntered into town crowned with ivy, carrying a massive ivy thyrsus, accompanied by prowling satyrs and revelers drunk on wine.

Over the years, Dionysus's cult had attracted many, though there remained some doubtful of his powers. Pentheus, king of Thebes, was such a doubter. People whispered about what went on in Dionysus's secret cult, his so-called mysteries. Rumors of the group included tales of sexual adventure more appropriate to a cult of Aphrodite. Most disconcerting to Pentheus was that recently the women of Thebes—upstanding women from respectable households—had left their looms and hearths to join the mysteries as maenads. They dressed up and ran into the forest of Mount Cithaeron—the same place where Actaeon had been killed by his own hunting hounds—to partake in the revelry, drinking and dancing and singing all night long. The women of Thebes ran giddily barefoot out of their homes and through the city gates, leaving husbands and children, propelled by Dionysus— hence his nickname, "woman-maddener." Even Pentheus's own mother and aunts had fallen prey.

Pentheus decided it was time to take action, and he locked up as many worshippers of Dionysus as possible in his palace. For good measure, he also imprisoned the priest of the strange cult. No sooner had he secured the locks, however, than the palace walls shuddered under a terrific thunderbolt, and smoke filled the air. The women's shackles sprang open, the doors slid apart, and the prisoners poured out.

Pentheus sprinted out of the palace only to find the priest standing outside, waiting for him. Pentheus demanded to know who had let him out. "Dionysus," replied the priest. Pentheus's snicker was interrupted by a herdsman who claimed he'd seen women in the forest wearing fawn skins and snakes, suckling wolves and deer, and drinking wine. They acted possessed, dancing and howling and ripping animals apart with their bare hands. Pentheus ordered the activities to stop.

"I must caution you," said the priest, "against interfering in the rites of the god."

Pentheus rolled his eyes. "What kind of rites are these? It doesn't sound much like sacred activity to me."

"What these women do is privy to the god Dionysus and to the initiated, no one else," replied the priest.

"Well," snorted Pentheus, "I'm not going to join the cult to find out."

"There might be another way," offered the priest. "Perhaps, if you're willing, you might accompany me. But you'll have to disguise yourself." He paused. "As a woman."

Pentheus had heard that the followers of Dionysus engaged in frenzied orgies and performed sexual acts of every kind. How could he resist this opportunity to observe?

What Pentheus didn't know was that he wasn't talking to a priest of Dionysus. He was talking to the god himself.

Bewigged and clad in a fawnskin dress, a barefoot Pentheus brandished his own thyrsus as the priest led him up Mount Cithaeron. They reached a clearing from where they could make out the festivities but remain hidden behind some trees.

Through the branches, Pentheus saw the women of Thebes quiver as they sang in the flickering shadows cast by moonlight and torch flame.

It was a good vantage point, but Pentheus still couldn't quite discern the scene below. "Pity I can't get a better view," he mused. His companion smiled and squinted his all-knowing eyes at the king. Grabbing hold of the nearest pine tree, Dionysus bent the trunk down to the ground.

"Here, Pentheus. Up top, you'll have a perfect view."

Pentheus planted himself atop the highest branch, and his friend let the tree slowly rise upright. Now Pentheus could see everything: his mother, his aunts, other Theban women, all clad in animal skins, laughing drunkenly. What the messenger said was true! They danced as if possessed, striking tambourines and playing flutes, throwing their heads back and spinning rhythmically. They were far too occupied to notice him, he said to himself with a chuckle.

Suddenly, a voice boomed from below. "There is a stranger in our midst. A spy! One who has scorned us. One who has mocked our sacred rituals. Punish him!"

Pentheus scanned the ground for help, but his guide had disappeared. The women spotted the interloper, plainly visible sitting on top of a tree. They raced up the hill toward Pentheus, who, petrified, clung tight to the branches. They threw pinecones and sticks at him and shook the tree but couldn't dislodge him. Together the women grabbed hold of the thick trunk, and with strength Pentheus had never seen before tore its roots right out of the earth and slammed it to the ground.

Surrounded by women foaming at the mouth, he ripped off his wig and shouted to his mother, Agave, "Look! It's me, your son, Pentheus! I was foolish to spy on you. But, please, have mercy! Don't kill me! I am your own son!" Agave, however, was not listening. She seized his hand, planted a heel on his chest, and yanked his arm straight out of its socket, tossing her head back with a shriek of delight. The women swarmed over him like ants, snatching pieces of his body—his feet, his hands, his ears—and clawing at his ribs. The countryside grew littered with pieces of Pentheus's body, as blood-soaked Theban women, possessed by mad Dionysus, cheered themselves on.

Agave led the triumphal procession down to the city, holding her thyrsus proudly ahead like a standard. As the women strode through the streets, Agave spotted her father, Cadmus.

"We women have taken up a new pursuit—the hunt," she cried. "I have slain a mountain lion with my bare hands. My first kill!"

Cadmus recoiled, seeing his daughter clad in splattered fawnskin, and knew Dionysus had been at work. He spoke solemnly. "Look again, Agave. What is perched atop your thyrsus? Is it the head of a mountain lion? Look again, Agave. Look again."

Only then did Agave cease to hear flutes and revelry. She heard only her heartbeat growing louder as her son's head came into focus before her.

KNOWING

OEDIPUS

The oracle of Apollo warned the king and queen of Thebes, Laius and Iocasta, not to have children, for any son born to them would kill his father. One evening, though, Laius got drunk and forgot—or maybe he was just seized with desire—and made love to his wife, who gave birth to a boy. Fearing the prophecy, they asked a shepherd to expose the baby on Mount Cithaeron. As an extra precaution, the man was to pin the baby's ankles together so it couldn't crawl to safety. While taking the baby out to a rocky cliff, the shepherd took pity on it and handed it off to another fellow who worked for the king and queen of Corinth. The childless couple was delighted to adopt it.

Thus Oedipus grew up as a prince in Corinth. When he was eighteen, a drunken dinner companion told Oedipus that the rulers of Corinth weren't really his parents. Oedipus shrugged the comment off as nonsense, but the more time passed, the more he thought about it. He traveled to Delphi and consulted the oracle of Apollo, who warned him not to return to his native land or he would murder his father and have sex with his mother. Oedipus, not daring to return to Corinth, had no choice but to make a new life elsewhere, far from his parents.

His chariot drove toward Thebes, where it reached a narrow crossroads at the same time as another chariot; both could not pass through at once. The other driver shouted for him to get out of the way, but Oedipus, full of princely arrogance, refused. The other man was so furious that he killed one of Oedipus's horses, and

Oedipus in turn killed both the driver and the passenger of the other chariot. Then he carried on to Thebes.

. . .

When Laius, king of Thebes, was killed, his brother Creon ascended the throne. Not long after, Hera sent a Sphinx to perch on a cliff near the city gates and ask a riddle of all who entered. It was said that if anyone could solve the riddle, Thebes would be rid of the Sphinx. An incorrect answer, however, would result in the traveler being eaten alive. So many visitors perished that Creon added extra incentive: Whoever solved the riddle would become king of Thebes and marry Laius's widow, Iocasta.

When Oedipus came to the gates of Thebes, the Sphinx posed her riddle: "What has four feet, two feet, and three feet but only one voice?"

"Man," wagered Oedipus. "Babies crawl, so they're four footed, adults walk on two feet, and the elderly use a cane—the third foot."

The Sphinx, shocked at the correct answer, threw herself to her death.

This was how Oedipus became king of Thebes and married Iocasta. They had two daughters and two sons and lived happily together until, years later, a plague descended on the region, bringing threat of famine. Oedipus consulted the oracle of Apollo, who revealed that something unclean polluted the land: To end the plague, it must be driven out. Clearly, the oracle referred to the killer of Laius, so Oedipus vowed to find and exile him.

He consulted the blind seer Tiresias but received only uncooperative replies. When Oedipus pressed him, Tiresias told him bluntly to stop questioning, but the king persisted.

"Oedipus, you want to know the killer of Laius?" he said quietly. "The killer you seek is yourself."

"That's impossible!" retorted Oedipus. "What do you know?"

Tiresias raised his eyebrows. "As you're such a master of riddles, Oedipus, here's another: Today is the day that will bring both your birth and your death."

Convinced that Tiresias was up to some kind of trickery, Oedipus consulted his wife about Laius's death. When she recounted how the king was murdered at a crossroads by an unknown assailant, Oedipus grew uneasy. But before he could ask anything else, a messenger interrupted them to announce the death of the king of Corinth. Oedipus let out a gleeful cry. When his wife remarked that it was a strange reaction for a son, Oedipus hastened to explain. His words tumbled out—the oracle from his youth, being fated to kill his father and marry his mother, and how he'd left Corinth.

"But now," he cried, "I've outwitted the gods! I've escaped my own fate!"

The messenger interrupted again. "You didn't have anything to worry about in the first place. The king and queen of Corinth weren't your real parents, anyway."

"Pardon me," said Oedipus with a sneer, "but just how do you know?"

The messenger explained that many years ago, a shepherd had given him a baby. Oedipus asked a few more questions and discovered that the messenger had in turn offered the baby to a childless couple. Iocasta, aghast, begged Oedipus to stop with his questions, but he did not relent. Finally, the messenger revealed that the couple in question had been the king and queen of Corinth. The messenger concluded, "They called you Oedipus, 'swollen foot,' because you'd had your feet pinned together."

They were interrupted by a second messenger, who brought news of Iocasta's death. In his pursuit of the truth, Oedipus had not noticed his wife's disappearance.

He ran into their bedroom, where Iocasta had hanged herself, and he ripped the broaches off her robe, jamming them into his eyes to blind himself. Then, obeying his own orders, he cast himself into exile.

Doesn't the saying go, "Ignorance is bliss"?

LAOCOÖN AND THE WOODEN HORSE

It was all Odysseus's idea. Odysseus the wily. Odysseus of the thousand ruses. Odysseus, that clever, lying fox.

Epeius built it, but not alone: He had the help of Athena in engineering the towering structure from Cretan timber outside the gates of Troy. Odysseus led the finest fighters inside and crawled in last of all, shutting the trapdoor in the great beast's side. On the horse's exterior, these words were inscribed: "An offering to Athena for a safe journey home."

The Achaeans burned their tents and boarded their ships, setting sail in the night. Only Sinon stayed at Troy, though not inside the horse, for he was to give the Greeks their signal to return.

The next morning, the Trojans discovered the Wooden Horse outside the city gates and found the Greek camp deserted. At last, those Greeks had given up! They'd set sail and returned home, their tails between their legs! "We have defeated the Greeks!" they cried. "Praise Troy, and praise the gods!"

The Trojans dragged the heavy beast with its silent stowage into the city. They piled wreaths of flowers round its neck and spread rose petals at its feet. They sacrificed to the gods and feasted on roasted meat and drank sweet wine late into the night, singing and dancing around the horse.

Only a few were suspicious—Cassandra, of course, and a seer, the priest of Apollo; yes, clear-sighted Laocoön knew. When the horse appeared, Laocoön tried to

warn his compatriots, but before he could speak, shepherds brought in a captive: a young Greek left behind, abandoned by his fellow men, now a prisoner of Troy.

Surrounded by a crowd of eager Trojans, Sinon lamented his fate. Telling them that Odysseus had turned against him and that he'd escaped from the Greeks, who wanted to sacrifice him to the gods, he begged the Trojans to have mercy on him.

Meanwhile, another crowd discussed how to destroy the horse. Some wanted to throw it over a cliff. Others suggested putting a torch to it. One man wanted to chop it to bits.

Laocoön, listening to all this, cried out over the chattering.

"How can you listen to Sinon and believe him? Will you not remember that he is a Greek and that, just like every Greek, he is a liar? Far-fetched is what I'd call his story. But Sinon is not the greatest liar of all. No, that man rests inside the Wooden Horse. That man, my friends, is Odysseus.

"Yes, inside your horse, around which you dance and sing, around whose neck you drape flowers and upon which you pour libations, inside lies our downfall. This horse is a trap!"

He was interrupted by a shout from the crowd, "So *serious,* Laocoön. Why can't you just enjoy this gift? After so many years of war, can't we have a little fun? Let's feast and get drunk and have a good time!"

"What madness has blinded you? Do you really trust Sinon to tell you the truth?" retorted the priest. "Are you telling me you trust a Greek, our enemy, over me, endowed with the grace of Apollo?"

Jeers from the crowd interrupted him again, so he turned and, with a groan, threw his spear at the side of the horse.

It resonated with a deep echo. Didn't anyone think it strange for the horse to echo?

"Inside that horse," Laocoön began again, "is—"

But before he could finish, a noise caused everyone to turn their heads. It was the sound of surf—no, of splashing—no, of slithering.

Two fanged serpents writhed out of the sea foam, heading across the sand toward Laocoön's sons, who stood not far away. The boys shrieked for help, and Laocoön jumped to their aid, beating the serpents with his fists as they wound themselves around his sons. When one bit him, he stumbled, and soon it had coiled itself around him, too. The serpents hissed and squeezed tighter around him and his sons, but no one came to their aid, for the Trojans believed the serpents were sent by Athena to punish Laocoön for injuring the Wooden Horse. Within minutes, the cries of the priest and his sons diminished as they suffocated.

That evening, while Troy slept, Sinon lit his fatal beacon on the grave of Achilles, alerting the Greek ships that hovered at the nearby island of Tenedos. Odysseus signaled to the men inside the horse, and they climbed out, heading straight to the city gates to let their comrades in.

The city awoke to a swarm of bloodthirsty Greeks.

And that was how the Trojan War was won.

TIRESIAS

One evening, while Zeus and Hera were dining, Zeus drank excessively of the nectar of the gods. "Hera," he slurred, "you know, women enjoy lovemaking more than men ever do."

Hera stiffened. "No, Zeus, men do. Or, at least, you must enjoy lovemaking an awful lot, or why would you always be on the prowl?"

Zeus was caught. It was true that Hera never strayed, but he couldn't believe his gender gained more pleasure in bed. Hera was equally unwavering in her opinion. Yet, as neither had any proof, the only way to solve the argument was to find someone who knew both sides of the story.

Enter Tiresias. His credentials were this: Walking in the mountains, he once saw a pair of snakes copulating right in the middle of the path. Tiresias stopped and thought for a moment. He could turn back, he could continue on his way and risk being bitten, or he could break the snakes apart. He opted for the latter and smacked them with his staff until the snakes decoupled, whereupon Tiresias was transformed into a woman.

Tiresias spent seven years in this state. He may have missed a few manly things, but lovemaking had taken on a whole new dimension. In his eighth year of womanhood, walking on that same wooded path, he found, as luck would have it, another pair of copulating snakes. "If striking snakes was so powerful the first time, why not try again?" Tiresias asked himself. As he broke the pair apart with his staff, he was transformed back into a man.

When he came before Zeus and Hera to answer that famous question, "Who enjoys lovemaking more?" Tiresias smiled and replied, "That's simple. A woman receives nine times as much pleasure from lovemaking as does a man."

Zeus let out a hearty chortle, but Hera, always a sore loser, struck Tiresias blind. Zeus pitied Tiresias's sightless state and offered him a gift. It was sight of a different sort—prophecy, the gift of prescient knowledge. This is why we call Tiresias "the blind seer."

JEALOUSY

HERA AND IO

Io was a nymph and a priestess of Hera. One day, Zeus spotted her, lovely, fair skinned, her hair dripping as she returned home from the river. Though Io fled, Zeus was quicker. Transforming himself into a thundercloud, he descended from the heavens like a thick fog and ravished her.

Hera thought it odd that dark clouds should appear so suddenly above a meadow while the sun shone bright at midday. Further, her husband was nowhere to be found. Suspecting Zeus was up to his usual antics, she descended to Earth.

After his many affairs, Zeus had grown wise about Hera's jealous intuition, so, anticipating her arrival, he turned Io into a cow. When Hera arrived, she greeted her husband primly, "Whose lovely milk-white heifer is this, dear, sweet husband? Is she from a mortal or immortal herd?"

Her question caught him off guard, for he hadn't prepared a full story. "She belongs to Earth," he blurted.

"Well, in that case, might I be so lucky as to have the heifer for myself? I mean, as it belongs to no one in particular . . ."

What could Zeus do? Giving his lover to Hera was outright betrayal, but refusing to do so was admitting guilt. Best to placate his wife, Zeus thought, and he handed the cow over.

Hera placed Io in a sacred grove, far from Zeus's gaze, and entrusted all-seeing Argos to watch over her. Argos's giant body was covered in eyes, and he needed no sleep, so he could watch Io constantly and from every angle.

Though Zeus had transformed Io into an exceptionally beautiful cow, she was a cow nonetheless. She had oafish cloven hooves where she'd had delicate fingers, and a plodding body when once she'd been lithe and graceful. She snorted inadvertently, and her nose was always wet. She spent her days wandering the riverbanks, her pendulous udder swaying, weeping great bovine tears and making the only sound she could, a mournful low. Taking pity on her, Zeus sent Hermes to her rescue. Hermes played his flute for Argos, lulling the monster to sleep, and cut off his head.

Argos's death left Io free to roam, but when Hera caught wind of Io's escape, she was furious. After placing all of Argos's eyes on the tail feathers of a bird—the peacock—she sent a gadfly to Io, for whom her husband undoubtedly still had a soft spot.

The gadfly was a source of constant irritation to Io, just as Zeus's philandering was to Hera. Io walked continually, blinking and swishing her tail, trying to rid herself of the fly. She even wondered whether the fly was the ghost of Argos, destined to pester her for eternity. Io wandered through northern Greece and swam across the Mediterranean, leaving her name on the Ionian Sea. She traversed Illyria and traveled past Mount Haemus. She entered the Caucasus Mountains, where she met Prometheus, who was being punished daily by Zeus's eagle. She ambled out of Europe into Asia, crossing the Bosporus, which was named after her (*Bosporus* means "cow's ford"). On and on Io walked, trying to lose the gadfly.

Finally, Zeus spotted Io in Egypt, pacing the banks of the Nile. When Hera wasn't looking, he came down and touched Io, transforming her back into a nymph. She then gave birth to a boy, Zeus's son, whom she named Epaphus ("touched").

Some say that wandering Io is like the moon, which travels across the sky night after night, watched from dusk to dawn by twinkling, sleepless eyes.

PROCRIS AND CEPHALUS

Procris and Cephalus of Athens married for love. Not too long after their wedding, Cephalus went hunting on Mount Hymettus. As Eos (Dawn) covered the sky with a glow, she spotted him, alone, striding across a dewy meadow on his way to the forest. "What man wouldn't wish to make love to a goddess every night?" thought Eos. As she watched him, she grew desirous.

"If Zeus can do it, so can I," she said to herself, and she swept Cephalus out of the forest and flew off.

There are few—if any—chances in life when a man can elope with a goddess, and Cephalus had just stumbled across his. But he was deeply in love with his wife, so what could have been a delightful tryst instead pained him.

"Eos, forgive me. You're everything a man could want, but I love my wife, Procris, and I can't bear to be without her. I must return."

"Fine," sniffed Eos. "Return to your Procris. Trust me, though—you'll wish you hadn't."

Cephalus returned home but found he couldn't dismiss Eos's words "You'll wish you hadn't." What did she mean? Did Eos know something he didn't? Was she referring to Procris being unfaithful?

Doubt found a permanent home in Cephalus. While his wife was away hunting, Cepahalus came to believe that she was enjoying multiple affairs. He tortured himself, imagining her making love to other men, and he considered confronting her, but he was sure she'd only lie.

He prayed for guidance, and of all the gods, Eos offered assistance. She encouraged him to leave home for a while and return to Athens disguised. Doing so, he found Procris morose and was so moved by her loyalty, so filled with desire, that he nearly revealed himself. But he refrained—he wasn't going to let emotion get in the way.

Cephalus became a frequent visitor to his unknowing wife, but she rejected his advances and insisted that she kept herself for one man alone. Most would be convinced at this point of their spouse's fidelity, but Cephalus was so certain of her wrongdoing that he thought he just hadn't set the right trap. Once he tried offering her money, but that didn't work either. He offered again, increasing the sum.

It went on like this for some time until, one day, Procris hesitated. Her pause was for but a split second, but it was all that was necessary for Cephalus: He had succeeded in cuckolding himself. When he removed his disguise, Procris was so appalled that she left him.

Procris devoted herself to the virgin goddess Artemis and lived among Artemis's fierce band of huntresses. In the months that followed, Cephalus regretted his jealous behavior and tried to find his wife. Artemis's band kept itself surprisingly scarce, however, for, as everyone knows, they avoid men.

By chance one day, Cephalus caught sight of Procris when she dismounted for a rest in the forest. Falling to his knees, he wept and begged her to return. She agreed.

When Cephalus thought back to Eos's words, he was relieved that her prediction had come and gone. How could he ever regret choosing Procris over Eos?

Cephalus hunted more successfully from then on, for Procris had given him a spear from Artemis that had impeccable aim. After lunch each day, he would lie down under a tree to enjoy the cool afternoon breeze. "Ah, Breeze!" he would sigh, "come here and caress me!"

Before long, word got back to Procris that her husband was having afternoon trysts with a nymph named Breeze. The jealous are always those who have something to hide, she thought, fuming.

When Cephalus left for his hunt the next morning, Procris followed him. After years of hunting with Artemis, she was so light-footed that she followed him the entire day undetected. When he lay down that afternoon under his favorite tree, sure enough, she heard those words: "Ah, Breeze, come here and caress me!"

Procris crept closer, holding her breath. But in her eagerness, she was not so quiet as before, and Cephalus heard the leaves rustle nearby. "A wild boar—what a triumph that would be!" he thought as he aimed his spear, the spear that never missed its target, into the undergrowth.

Cephalus recognized his wife's shriek and scrambled under the bushes, where he found her wounded.

"Cephalus," she whispered, "promise you'll never dishonor me by marrying Breeze."

He never had time to explain.

GREED

MIDAS

One hot afternoon, as Dionysus and his unruly band ambled along, one reveler, old Silenus, fell behind, exhausted or just plain drunk. When he sat down to rest, he was kidnapped by a band of peasants who brought him to the king of Phrygia, Midas.

Midas, initiated into the mysteries of Dionysus, immediately recognized Silenus, and he celebrated the old satyr's visit with ten days of elaborate festivities. On the eleventh day he accompanied Silenus on his journey to Lydia to rejoin the god.

Dionysus was so impressed with Midas's generosity that he offered the king a reward. "Anything you please," said the god. However, when he saw Midas's expression change, Dionysus knew he had misspoken.

Although Midas lived in luxury as a king, or perhaps because of it, the first thing that came to his mind was gold. He didn't want a finite sum, though—better to have a continual supply. He asked Dionysus that everything he touch turn into gold. Dionysus, the god of excess and encourager of wild activities, nonetheless knew that sometimes moderation is appropriate. But having promised, he had no choice but to grant Midas his wish.

As Midas made his way home, he touched a tree to test his wish. Sure enough, the branch turned to gold along with all of its leaves. He snapped off the branch and put it in his pocket, turning that to gold as well. When he ran his hand through the dirt, gold dust sifted through his fingers. When he caressed the stalks of grain in a field, he left a row of golden sheaves glistening in the sun. When he picked an apple from a tree, he held a golden fruit that could have fooled anyone into believing it belonged to the Hesperides.

When Midas returned home, he turned his palace into gold by touching the doorposts. He would live his days in a golden palace! Midas was drunk on his newfound source of riches. He'd be the richest man in the world! It was too good to be true!

The excitement left Midas famished, so he sat down to dinner. He shoveled a forkful of roasted meat to his lips but found that upon contact the meat turned to gold. He ripped off a hunk of bread but the bread became a golden lump. He took a swig of wine but spat out liquid gold.

Only then did Midas realize the futility of his wish. No amount of the gold in the world could feed him. He traveled to Lydia to confess his greed to Dionysus and beg forgiveness. To his surprise, Dionysus took pity on him and told him where to find a mountain spring that would purify him.

After Midas was rid of his luxurious curse, he lived frugally in the mountains as a hermit.

HUBRIS

ARACHNE

Arachne was renowned throughout Lydia for her weaving. It was said that nymphs came down from the mountains and out of the rivers just to watch her fingers dance over the yarn. She was so gifted, people speculated that Athena had bestowed talent upon her.

Arachne bristled at the idea that her skill was not her own. She was certain, moreover, that she wove better than the goddess did and declared a contest between them. "If I lose," Arachne challenged, "Athena may do with me what she pleases."

Not long after, an old, arthritic woman visited Arachne at her loom. "I hear you've challenged Athena to a weaving contest," she said. "Let me give you a suggestion: Compete with your fellow mortals instead and apologize to the goddess. Athena will still forgive you for your hubris."

Arachne scoffed. "Stupid woman! If Athena's so great, and if she truly can't be beaten, then why doesn't she come to Lydia herself? It's nothing but cowardice."

Athena's fury broke through her disguise, and everyone around paid homage—except Arachne, who held her head high despite a deep blush that crept over her cheeks.

Two looms were set up in parallel so Athena and Arachne could see each other's progress. They began to weave, warp, and woof, using wine-colored yarn and yarn of Phoenician purple, yarn the color of the afternoon sun, of chestnuts, and of the dark, stormy sea. A thousand colors they wove, blending them deftly to tell stories.

Athena depicted her victory over Poseidon to become patron of Athens. She wove the image of herself plunging her spear into the ground on the Acropolis and the olive tree that sprang forth. In the corners of her tapestry, Athena wove other contests of mortals against gods: Rhodope and Haemus, turned into mountains for calling themselves by the gods' names, and Antigone, transformed into a stork after challenging Hera.

Arachne wove stories of the gods' exploits and their deceptions of mortals. For instance, she wove the loves of Zeus: when he disguised himself as a bull to abduct Europa, as a swan to seduce Leda, as golden rain to impregnate Danaë. She wove loves of the other gods, too: Poseideon transformed as a dolphin to seduce Melantho, Apollo disguised as a shepherd to make love to Isse.

Athena inspected her competitor's finished work, and finding it faultless, ripped it apart and beat Arachne with her weaving shuttle. Arachne, humiliated and bereft of the congratulations she felt she'd earned, prepared to hang herself, but Athena felt this was too generous an end, so she cursed Arachne:

"May you always hang and never stop weaving, and may all of your descendants have the same fate."

That is how spiders came to be.

MARSYAS

Athena played the two-piped flute wherever she went, leaving a trail of melodies behind her. One day, she caught sight of herself reflected in a stream as she played. Her cheeks were puffed out with air, distorting her whole face. Here she'd been, strolling around looking ridiculous for everyone to see! Disgusted, she threw down the flute, cursing it, and stormed off.

The flute remained on the forest floor for days until a satyr named Marsyas stumbled across it. When he picked it up and blew, to his delight the flute made melodious sounds. Soon, Marsyas had mastered a repertoire. He played for the birds, for the frogs, for the sun, and for the wind. Unconcerned with puffy cheeks—satyrs aren't renowned for their good looks, anyhow—Marsyas played the flute to his heart's content.

Marsyas grew so pleased with himself that he began to brag. "I'm the best player there is!" he announced to his audiences. Confident he was a superior musician to even Apollo, he challenged the god to a contest in which the loser's punishment would be at the discretion of the winner.

The Muses served as judges, listening to Marsyas first. Never had they heard such pleasing notes as those that arose from the satyr's flute! He was undoubtedly the winner, but out of respect, they listened to Apollo, too. Apollo's lyre playing was pleasant, to be sure, but it was nothing extraordinary. Then came Apollo's lilting voice, harmonizing with the notes from his lyre, and the Muses, stunned, voted unanimously in favor of Apollo.

Marsyas was shocked. Apollo, in his opinion, had cheated: He'd played an instrument *and* sang. It just wasn't fair! As he stood there fuming, the god came over and placed a hand on his shoulder.

"What punishment fits this crime of hubris?" Apollo asked softly, smiling. "What made you think you could possibly play better than an immortal, better than Apollo, son of Leto? It's futile to challenge the gods, Marsyas, for we will always win."

As Apollo tied Marsyas's wrists and ankles, the satyr let his chin sink to his chest. Apollo pulled his arms high above his head, stretching his skin taut like the strings of a lyre, and bound him to a tree. Marsyas wept, knowing he would die there in that very spot, abandoned.

A glimmer caught Marsyas's eye. Apollo's Scythian accomplice crouched nearby, sharpening a blade in the hot sun. Marsyas thanked the gods for granting him a quick and merciful death.

He was wrong. Marsyas's punishment for challenging Apollo was this: He was flayed alive, his skin peeled from him, till all his muscles were displayed. Everyone mourned his death—all the other satyrs, and the nymphs and the shepherds, and all the musical creatures, too: The birds sang sorrowfully, the bees grew quiet, and the crickets chirped only a few solemn notes. All these creatures wept for miles around when they heard of poor, proud Marsyas's fate, so much that their tears pooled together and formed a river, which they named after him.

Marsyas's skin was displayed for all to see in the market in Celaenae, as a reminder.

HEROISM

PERSEUS AND MEDUSA

An oracle told Acrisius of Argos that any son born to his daughter Danaë would grow up to kill him. Determined to outwit fate, he locked his daughter in a bronze underground chamber so that she would never get married and certainly never become pregnant. Zeus, however, seeing Danaë chaste, lovely, and alone, entered the chamber as golden rain and made love to her.

When Acrisius heard the cries of an infant from his daughter's room, he ordered Danaë and baby Perseus locked in a chest and cast out to sea, but they were rescued by a fisherman from the island of Seriphus.

Even after Perseus grew up, his mother's beauty continued to get her into trouble. When Perseus was a young man, the king of Seriphus, an unsavory fellow called Polydectes, desired her. But as Polydectes couldn't seduce Danaë with Perseus around, the king concocted a plan to dispose of him.

Polydectes announced he wished to marry a girl named Hippodamia. As was customary, his subjects gave gifts to help him woo his future bride and impress her parents. Although everyone else announced horses as their gifts, Perseus offered to give Polydectes the head of Medusa, one of the deadly Gorgons, horrible winged creatures with snakes for hair and teeth like a wild boar's. It was a strange suggestion. But for Polydectes, it was perfect, for the errand would take the boy a very long time—if he returned at all. In the meantime, he could set about pursuing Danaë.

Perseus was soon on his way. He had first to find the nymphs, for they had gifts to give him, but he needed directions, so he visited the sisters of the Gorgons, a trio known as the Graeae, gray haired since birth. The sisters shared a single eye and a single tooth, which enabled them to better attack and eat visitors: Their eye never slept, and they could all partake of the feast. Perseus promptly took the eye and the tooth and demanded they tell him where to find a certain group of nymphs who had gifts for him. The blind and toothless Graeae complied. When he reached the nymphs, he received an invisibility cap belonging to Hades, a leather pouch, and a pair of winged sandals. Then, Hermes gave Perseus a sickle, and Athena gave him a polished bronze shield.

Fully equipped, Perseus set off for the Gorgons. He found them sleeping, which gave him time to craft a plan, for only one of the three—Medusa—was mortal and as everyone knows, you can't look straight at a Gorgon, for its eyes will turn you to stone. Perseus angled his shield to make out their reflections, and Athena guided his hand to select the mortal monster. After Perseus cut off Medusa's head, he tossed it in his leather pouch; from the drops of Medusa's blood were born two creatures: Chrysaor and the winged horse Pegasus. Medusa's sisters pursued him, but invisible in Hades' cap and flying swiftly in the winged sandals, he easily escaped.

On his way home, Perseus got sidetracked, as heroes often do, by an attractive young woman. Named Andromeda, she was chained to a cliff to be devoured by a sea monster. Perseus consulted the girl's father, the king of Ethiopia, who explained that it was foretold that the sacrifice of his daughter would end a plague on the land. Perseus persuaded the king to let him rescue Andromeda and marry her.

As the sea monster approached, Perseus flew into the air, casting his shadow on the sea. When the monster attacked the shadow, Perseus descended and stabbed it to death. As he rested on the beach with Andromeda, he absentmindedly set the Gorgon's head on a bed of seaweed, and its gaze turned the seaweed into coral.

Andromeda's father had failed to mention that she was betrothed to another man, Phineus, who was furious when he heard about Perseus and wanted to kill him. Perseus preempted Phineus by showing him the Gorgon's head and, hence, turning him to stone. Finally, Perseus returned home with Andromeda and the head of Medusa, only to discover his mother and the fisherman who had rescued them years before hiding in the temple in fear of Polydectes. Perseus knew it was time for revenge.

Striding into the king's palace, he announced, "I have an engagement gift for you, Polydectes: the head of the Gorgon Medusa."

Polydectes scoffed that this couldn't possibly be true, so Perseus took the head out of the bag. Polydectes and his court were immediately petrified.

Perseus left Seriphus, and the Gorgon's head having done its job, he gave it to Athena, who placed it in the middle of her aegis, making her more fearsome in battle than ever before.

And the prophecy?

When Acrisius heard of Perseus's existence, he left Argos for Larissa, in case his grandson came looking for him. Perseus, ignorant of Acrisius's flight, did in fact set out for Argos. On his way, he stopped at funeral games being held in Larissa to compete in the pentathlon. When Perseus threw the discus, a strong wind blew it off course. It struck Acrisius, killing him immediately.

THE LABORS OF HERACLES

Heracles was born to Alcmene and great-thundering Zeus after the king of the gods, disguised as Alcmene's husband on their wedding night, stole into her bridal chamber. Hera, furious with Zeus for indulging in yet another affair, sent snakes to the crib Heracles shared with his half-brother, but Heracles stood up and strangled them; the other child hid.

As a boy, Heracles learned how to drive a chariot, wrestle, master archery, engage in armed combat, and play the lyre, but he was unfortunately best known for his temper. After he killed his lyre teacher in frustration, Heracles was sent to tend the cattle of Thespius. When a lion attacked Thespius's cattle, Heracles killed it; thereafter, he wore the lion's skin, its head gaping toothily round his own.

As a young man Heracles was eight feet tall and stronger, faster, and bolder than anyone else. All the gods favored him: Hermes gave him a sword, Apollo a bow and quiver, Hephaestus a golden breastplate, and Athena a robe. Only Hera disliked Heracles, so she struck him temporarily mad, and he killed his wife and children.

When he realized his crime, he cast himself into exile and visited the oracle of Apollo at Delphi to learn how to purify himself. The oracle told him to go work for Eurystheus, king of Mycenae, in Tiryns, as penance.

Eurystheus gave Heracles the most difficult task he could think of: to bring him the skin of the Nemean lion. Having killed the Thespian lion, Heracles was confident he could do it, but the arrows he shot at the lion were ineffective. He cut a club from the trunk of an olive tree and studded it with bronze, and when the lion entered its den, Heracles blocked the entrance and came in through the exit, cornering it. The lion was so surprised that Heracles was able to strangle it with his bare hands.

Eurystheus, shocked by Heracles' fearlessness and strength, asked him not to come into town, but to announce his feats at the city gates. The king then sent Heracles away on another labor and constructed a huge bronze jar in which to hide.

Heracles' next task was to kill the Lernaean Hydra, a nine-headed monster with only one mortal head. Each time he guessed wrong and clubbed an immortal head, it grew back and become inseparable from the rest. So Heracles enlisted Iolus to stand by with a torch: As soon as he cut off an immortal head, Iolus cauterized the wound to prevent it from growing back. Heracles finally cut off the mortal head and dipped his arrows in the Hydra's poisonous bile. When Heracles returned to Tiryns, however, Eurystheus claimed that because Heracles had help, the labor didn't count.

Heracles was next called on to capture the golden-horned Cerynian hind sacred to Artemis, and bring it back alive. For an entire year Heracles chased the hind, until both were exhausted. He shot it with a single arrow to injure it, but as he was carrying it off, he was apprehended by Artemis and Apollo. When Heracles explained that he was indentured to Eurystheus, who had ordered him to capture it, they believed him and let him go.

For the fourth labor, Eurystheus sent Heracles to fetch the Erymanthian boar. Using his strategy with the hind, he chased the boar until it grew tired, and then he tied it up and brought it back to Eurystheus. (You may be wondering what Eurystheus planned to do with all of these animals—nobody knows.)

Eurystheus then ordered Heracles to clean the stables of Augeas in a single day. This seemed feasible until Heracles found out that Augeas owned more herds of cattle than he could count. Heracles told Augeas that he'd clean the stables in a day if Augeas would give him a tenth of his herds. Augeas, skeptical Heracles could do it, shrugged and agreed, and Heracles dug a channel across the stable yard to join two nearby rivers, flooding Augeas's land and washing away all the manure. When Augeas discovered that Heracles had done the task for Eurystheus, he refused to pay him, and when Eurystheus found out that Heracles had agreed to do it for profit, he refused to count it as a labor.

Heracles' next assignment was to drive the Stymphalian birds out of the forest where they flocked. The birds smelled so vile that he couldn't get near enough to shoo them away, and Heracles was stumped until Athena gave him a whistle. He blew it, frightening the birds, and they flew off.

For the seventh labor, Eurystheus asked Heracles to bring him the Cretan bull, the one that Pasiphae, wife of Minos, loved. After Heracles brought it back, Eurystheus, perhaps because of his growing collection of stolen animals, ordered it let free, and it roamed until it got to Marathon, where it attacked the inhabitants. Theseus later killed it.

Labor number eight was to bring Eurystheus the man-eating mares of Diomedes, king of the Bistones. Heracles overthrew the stable hands and led the mares to his ship, but just as he was departing, the Bistones attacked. Heracles told his lover, Abderus, to watch over the mares, but they tore him to bits. Heracles fought off the Bistones, killed Diomedes, and buried what remained of Abderus. After he showed the mares to Eurystheus, he let them go; they were later killed by wild animals on Mount Olympus.

Eurystheus next asked Heracles to bring him the belt of Hippolyte, queen of the Amazons—fierce female warriors who reared only girls and cut off their right breasts so that they could throw javelins unencumbered. When Heracles arrived, Hippolyte met him at his ship and gladly agreed to give him her belt, but before she'd taken it off, Hera, disguised as an Amazon, spread a rumor that Heracles intended to kidnap Hippolyte. The Amazons raced toward Heracles' ship, so he, thinking they were attacking, killed Hippolyte, took her belt, and fled.

When Heracles presented the belt to Eurystheus, he was charged with another labor: to bring back the cattle of Geryon, creatures with a single head but three bodies. After all his labors, Heracles thought, how hard could herding cattle be?

He traveled across Europe to Libya, where, hot and irritable, he shot an arrow at Helios (the Sun). Helios, impressed with Heracles' courage, lent him his golden cup to cross the sea to the island of Erythia, where Geryon lived. Geryon caught Heracles leading off his cattle, so Heracles killed him and loaded the cattle into Helios's great golden cup. On his way back to Tiryns, Poseidon's two sons tried to steal the cows, so Heracles slew them, too. In southern Italy, one of the bulls ran off and swam to Sicily, where Heracles found it mixed up with Eryx's herds, but Eryx wouldn't give it back until Heracles agreed to a wrestling match. Heracles won, killing Eryx, and brought the bull back to the herd. Now, all he had to do was drive them back to Mycenae, but Hera sent gadflies that drove the cows berserk, and they ran off into the Thracian foothills. He rounded up as many as he could (would Eurystheus know the difference?), and Eurystheus sacrificed them to Hera.

Eight years and a month, and ten labors—you'd think Eurystheus would be satisfied, but he still refused to count the killing of the Hydra and the cleaning of the Augean stables, so Heracles had two more labors to go.

Labor eleven was to retrieve the famous golden apples of the Hesperides, daughters of Nyx (Night) who lived in Libya, not far from where the Titan Atlas held up the sphere of the heavens. A hundred-headed serpent that never slept guarded the magical, fertile, and immortal apples, which hung from a tree that it was said Gaia (Earth) had given Hera as a wedding gift.

Heracles asked Atlas to fetch three apples while he took the Titan's place holding up the heavens. When Atlas returned, he told Heracles he'd give the apples to Eurystheus, for secretly he was tired of supporting the heavens. Heracles thanked him for the offer and asked Atlas if before he left, he couldn't hold the heavens again for a moment so that Heracles could put a pillow against his head to ease the burden. Atlas complied, but Heracles picked up the apples and walked off, leaving Atlas stuck. When Heracles gave the apples to Eurystheus, the king, perhaps tired of gifts, gave them right back, so Heracles offered them to Athena.

For the hero's last labor, Eurystheus ordered Heracles to bring him Cerberus, the three-headed serpent-tailed dog that guards the gates of the Underworld. When Heracles asked Hades whether he might take Cerberus for a walk, Hades agreed, with a chuckle, that it was fine as long as Heracles didn't use any weapons.

With nothing but a breastplate and a lion skin to protect him, Heracles strode up to the dog and put a stranglehold on it. He held on tight, even after Cerberus's tail bit him, and the dog grew submissive. After showing the dog to Eurystheus, he was glad to return Cerberus to Hades.

Having braved the most treacherous land of all, the Underworld, Heracles was released from servitude. But his accomplishments didn't stop there: He helped the Greeks fight in Troy, joined Jason and the Argonauts to retrieve the Golden Fleece, and founded the Olympic Games.

As every hero's story must have an end, here is that of Heracles: He accepted help from a centaur named Nessus to cross a river by giving his wife, Deianira, to Nessus to carry. When the centaur—which everyone knows is a lascivious creature—reached the far bank, it tried to rape her, so Heracles shot it with an arrow. Before Nessus died, he told Deianira to mix some of his blood shed from Heracles' arrow and some of his sperm spilled on the earth to form a love potion.

Years later, Deianira heard a rumor that Heracles was in love with another woman, so she soaked a robe in the potion to win him back. As soon as he put it on, though, Heracles began to writhe—for, unbeknownst to Deianira, Nessus's blood had been tinged by the poison of the Lernaean Hydra on Heracles' arrow tip. Heracles tried to take the robe off, but it stuck to him, and when he tugged, some of his flesh came off. As the poison sank deeper, Heracles' pain became insufferable, and seeking a quick end, he made his way to Mount Oeta, built a funeral pyre, and flung himself on top.

As the fire burned, smoke rose high and swept Heracles up to Mount Olympus. Zeus bestowed immortality upon him and gave him a new wife, Hebe (Youth).

And that is the story of Heracles, the greatest hero of the Greeks, and the only mortal to ever become a god.

GLOSSARY

ACHAEAN Achaea was the northwestern region of the Peloponnese; Homer uses the term Achaeans to refer to the Greeks (as opposed to the Trojans) in his tales of the Trojan War.

AEGIS A shield with scales and snake-head tassels and decorated with a Gorgon's head in the center; most commonly worn by Athena or Zeus.

CENTAUR A notoriously lascivious and uncivilized creature with the torso of a man and the body and legs of a horse.

DIADEM A royal headband akin to a crown.

HUBRIS Excessive pride or confidence; arrogance; the crime of dishonoring or acting insolently to one's superiors, primarily, the gods.

LYRE A musical instrument with seven strings, made of wood or tortoiseshell; invented by Hermes and played by Apollo.

MAENAD A female worshipper of Dionysus who, under the influence of the god, achieved a certain frenzied ecstasy.

METIS Wisdom, cunning, craft, skill, ingenuity. Also, the personification of intelligence (Zeus's first wife).

MYSTERIES Secret cults involving some form of initiation and communion with a god, sometimes through ecstasy (a sort of divine madness).

NYMPHS Young female divinities, sometimes considered daughters of Zeus, who lived in and hence were identified with trees, mountains, caves, or bodies of water (springs and rivers).

OLYMPIANS Residents of Mount Olympus, i.e., the gods.

ORACLE A sacred site from which a god responded to human questions; also, the pronouncement of such a response. The most important oracle in Greece was that of Apollo in Delphi (also called the Delphic oracle), thought to be located at the *omphalos*, or center of the universe; visitors seeking answers paid a tax and sacrificed before the Pythia, a woman, possessed by Apollo and crowned with laurel leaves, who sat on a tripod to relate his prophecies.

PARTHENOS An unmarried girl; a virgin; often an epithet of Athena.

PENTATHLON A contest comprising running, jumping, discus and javelin throwing, and wrestling.

PERSONIFICATION The embodiment of a concept or an element of the natural world; for instance, Peitho was the personification of persuasion, Pothos of longing, and so forth.

PURIFICATION In preparation for religious activity or in the case of pollution, a person might purify himself or herself through ritual washing, sacrifice (particularly of an animal), or fasting; more serious cases (such as murder) might require exile.

SACRIFICE An important aspect of Greek religion: Requests, thanks, and honor all required sacrifice to the gods; items sacrificed might include liquids (called libations), cereals, or animals. After animal sacrifice, the bones and fat were burned on an altar for the gods, and humans cooked the meat and ate it. Human sacrifice occurred only in myth.

SATYR A half-man, half-goat (sometimes half-horse) consort of Dionysus known for its appetite for wine and sex and often depicted with a large, erect phallus; sometimes called a silen.

SEER A prophet or fortune-teller. Interpreting dreams, observing birds and omens, and sacrificing animals were all methods of telling the future.

THYRSUS A pole wrapped with ivy or grapevines and with a pinecone on top to resemble a phallus; carried by worshippers of Dionysus.

THE UNDERWORLD The final resting place of the dead, presided over by Hades and Persephone and guarded by the three-headed dog Cerberus. Imagined as dark and musty, the Underworld was demarcated by the Acheron, Styx, Cocytus, and Lethe rivers. Ghosts were sometimes subjected to eternal torture there. To be admitted to the Underworld, the dead had to receive a proper burial.

THE ANCIENT MEDITERRANEAN (WITH MYTHICAL LOCATIONS)

SCYTHIA

CAUCASUS MTS.

Black Sea
(Euxine Sea)

MT. HAEMUS

COLCHIS

THRACE

ROME

Bosporus

CELAENAE

ASIA MINOR

ERYTHIA

SYRIA

SICILY
(LAND OF THE CYCLOPES)

CARTHAGE

CRETE

CYPRUS

Mediterranean Sea

PHOENICIA

JERUSALEM

LIBYA

Nile R.

GARDEN OF THE HESPERIDES

EGYPT

Red Sea

N
W   E
S

ETHIOPIA

ANCIENT GREECE AND THE AEGEAN (WITH MYTHICAL LOCATIONS)

THRACE

ILLYRIA

MT. OLYMPUS ▲

THESSALY

IOLCUS •

PHRYGIA

TENEDOS   • TROY

LAND OF
THE AMAZONS

MT. OETA ▲

Aegean Sea

• LARISSA

ITHACA

DELPHI •

• THEBES

LYDIA

ACHAEA   MT. CITHAERON ▲   ELEUSIS •

MT. ERYMANTHUS ▲   • MARATHON

MT. CYLLENE ▲   CORINTH •   ATHENS •

NEMEA •   ▲ MT. HYMETTUS

ARGOS •   • MYCENAE

OLYMPIA •   LERNA •   • TIRYNS

SAMOS •

DELOS •

ICARIA

Ionian Sea   • PYLOS   • SPARTA

CYCLADES IS.

SERIPHUS   NAXOS

TAENARUM (ENTRANCE TO THE UNDERWORLD)

Cretan Sea

CRETE

▲ MT. IDA

SELECTED BIBLIOGRAPHY

Before you consult any modern handbook, go straight to the ancient sources. Following is a list of easily accessible Greek and Roman texts (this is not a comprehensive list).

ODYSSEUS AND THE CYCLOPS
Homer *Odyssey* 9.105ff.

THE BIRTH OF ATHENA
Apollodorus *Library* 1.3.6
Hesiod *Theogony* 886–900
Lucian *Dialogues of the Gods* 8

HERMES AND APOLLO
Homeric *Hymn* 4, to Hermes
Apollodorus *Library* 3.10.2

THE MINOTAUR
Apollodorus *Library* 3.1.3–4, 3.16.7
Catullus *Carmina* 64.52–264
Plutarch *Theseus* 15–20
Ovid *Metamorphoses* 8.115–182

HELEN AND PARIS
Apollodorus *Library* Epitome
  3.1–7, 3.10.4–9, Epitome
  6.29–30
Lucian *Dialogues of the Gods* 20
Homer *Iliad* esp. 3
Homer *Odyssey* 4.230–305
Herodotus *Histories* 2.112–120

PYGMALION
Ovid *Metamorphoses* 10.243ff.
Ovid *History of Love* 4.1ff.

ICARUS
Apollodorus *Library* 3.16.12–13
Ovid *Metamorphoses* 8.183–235
Ovid *Art of Love* 2.19–98

ECHO AND NARCISSUS
Ovid *Metamorphoses* 3.341ff.
Ovid *History of Love* 15.1ff.

TANTALUS
Apollodorus *Library* Epitome
  2.1–3
Homer *Odyssey* 11.582–592
Pindar *Olympian* 1

PROMETHEUS
Hesiod *Theogony* 506–616
Hesiod *Works and Days* 53–105
Apollodorus *Library* 1.7.1
Aeschylus *Prometheus Bound*

MEDEA
Euripides *Medea*
Apollodorus *Library* 1.9.23–28
Apollonius Rhodius *Argonautica*
  esp. 3–4

DEMETER AND PERSEPHONE
Homeric *Hymn* 2, to Demeter
Ovid *Metamorphoses* 5.341–571

AJAX AND THE CONTEST OF ARMS

Pindar Nemian 7.20–30 and
 8.21–27
Apollodorus Library Epitome
 5.6–8
Sophocles Ajax
Ovid Metamorphoses 13.1–398

ORPHEUS AND EURYDICE

Virgil Fourth Georgic 453–527
Ovid Metamorphoses 10.1–85
Ovid History of Love 10.1ff.

PENTHEUS

Euripides Bacchae
Ovid Metamorphoses 3.511–733

OEDIPUS

Sophocles King Oedipus
Apollodorus Library 3.5.7–9

LAOCOÖN AND THE WOODEN HORSE

Apollodorus Library Epitome
 5.14–19
Virgil Aeneid 2.20ff.

TIRESIAS

Apollodorus Library 3.6.7
Ovid Metamorphoses 3.316–338

HERA AND IO

Apollodorus Library 2.1.3
Bacchylides Odes 19
Ovid Metamorphoses 1.583–746

PROCRIS AND CEPHALUS

Ovid Metamorphoses 7.690–865
Ovid History of Love 8.1ff.

MIDAS

Ovid Metamorphoses 11.90–193

ARACHNE

Ovid Metamorphoses 6.1–145

MARSYAS

Apollodorus Library 1.4.2
Ovid Metamorphoses 6.383–95

PERSEUS AND MEDUSA

Apollodorus Library 2.4.2–2.4.4
Ovid Metamorphoses 4.604–803,
 5.1–5.249

THE LABORS OF HERACLES

Apollodorus Library 2.4.8–2.7.8
Euripides Heracles esp. 359–424
 and 1265–78
Ovid Metamorphoses 9.98–272
Virgil Aeneid 8.175–279

EXPLORING FURTHER

If you find yourself wanting to know more, here are a few suggestions to get you started on your own mythological odyssey.

The *Oxford Classical Dictionary of Myth and Religion* should be your first stop as a reference work. It covers Greco-Roman as well as Judeo-Christian mythology and provides a short bibliography after each entry. Its predecessor, *The Oxford Classical Dictionary*, is the granddaddy of all classical reference works, a broader reference tool that covers the entire classical world. *The Genealogy of Greek Mythology* (New York: Gotham, 2003), by Vanessa James, is a comprehensive, illustrated foldout chart of mortal and immortal families. Consult Timothy Gantz's two-volume powerhouse *Early Greek Myth: A Guide to Literary and Artistic Sources* (Baltimore and London: Johns Hopkins University Press, 1993) for in-depth coverage.

For ancient sources, consult the Loeb Classical Library, a complete set of standard translations of well-known ancient authors as well as some more obscure bits and pieces. Volumes feature both the original language and English translation on facing pages. (Red volumes are works in Latin; green are works in Greek.)

Many ancient texts are also online in the Perseus Digital Library (www.perseus.tufts.edu). You can use the Web site's search engine to search by keyword within individual texts. The Perseus Library also features an impressive array of images of ancient art.

Apollodorus's *Library* is a compendium of the Greek myths mistakenly attributed to the Athenian Apollodorus. Never mind the attribution: The *Library* is a fabulous read. See Michael Simpson's translation, *Gods and Heroes of the Greeks: The Library of Apollodorus* (2nd edition, Amherst: University of Massachusetts Press, 1986); his notes are a rich source of detail and bibliography.

Ovid was a Roman poet who retold many Greek myths. Ted Hughes's lyrical translation of Ovid's *Metamorphoses*, entitled *Tales from Ovid* (New York: Farrar, Straus and Giroux, 1999), is delightful, though not literal. For a more standard version, see Michael Simpson's *The Metamorphoses of Ovid* (Amherst: University of Massachusetts Press, 2001), with its copious notes.

Homer was the author of two epic poems, *The Iliad* and *The Odyssey*, which date to the second half of the eighth century BC. (This attribution is still debated, however: Some believe the poems are compilations from a number of authors who recited them aloud over the years, and others believe they are the work of a single master.) If you've never read Homer's *Odyssey*, go out and buy yourself a copy right now—it's a fantastic story. Try translations of both poems by Richmond Lattimore (Chicago: University of Chicago Press, 1961; New York: Perennial, 1999) or Robert Fagles (New York: Penguin, 1998; New York: Penguin, 1999).

The *Homeric Hymns* were long attributed to Homer, but they are now accepted to be a collection of songs to the gods by a variety of poets composed in the seventh century BC. Try translations by Jules Cashford (London: Penguin, 2003) or Thelma Sargent (New York: W. W. Norton, 1975).

The poet Hesiod lived around 700 BC. His *Theogony* tells the origin of the gods and the universe and their genealogy; *Works and Days* is a collection of practical and moral advice. See M. L. West's translation as a single volume (Oxford: Oxford University Press, 1999).

Standard handbooks of classical myth include H. J. Rose's *A Handbook of Greek Mythology* (New York: Routledge, 1991); Barry Powell's *Classical Myth* (3rd edition, Upper Saddle River, N.J.: Prentice-Hall, 2001), and Robert Graves' *Greek Myths* (illustrated edition, London: Penguin, 1981). You may also have encountered Bulfinch's *Mythology* (New York: Modern Library: 1993), by Thomas Bulfinch, and *Mythology: Timeless Tales of Gods and Heroes* (New York: Warner, 1999), by Edith Hamilton. Richard P. Martin's *Myths of the Ancient Greeks* (New York: New American Library, 2003) provides a terrific introduction to the study of myth, and his retellings are a pleasure. Jean-Pierre Vernant's *The Universe, the Gods, and Men: Ancient Greek Myths*, translated by Linda Asher

(New York: Perennial, 2002), is great storytelling. Don't miss Charles Rowan Beye's *Odysseus: A Life* (New York: Hyperion, 2004), a quasi-novel that brings the ancient hero to life.

If you're interested in the interpretation and study of myth, take a look at Vernant's *Mortals and Immortals* (Princeton, N.J.: Princeton University Press, 1991), Mary Lefkowitz's *Greek Gods, Human Lives: What Greek Myths Can Teach Us* (New Haven, Conn.: Yale University Press, 2003), and Yves Bonnefoy's *Greek and Egyptian Mythologies* (Chicago and London: University of Chicago Press, 1992).

For learning about classical history, you might start with John Camp and Elizabeth Fisher's illustrated *The World of the Ancient Greeks* (New York: Thames & Hudson, 2002). John Boardman, Jasper Griffin, and Oswin Murray's *The Oxford Illustrated History of Greece and the Hellenistic World* is more in-depth and an excellent resource (Oxford: Oxford University Press, 2001). If you've ever felt that the classics are irrelevant, read Bernard Knox's *Oldest Dead White European Males* (New York: W. W. Norton, 1993). It will change your mind.

Art—both ancient and modern—can enrich your knowledge and enjoyment of myth. Greek sculpture and vase painting, and Roman wall painting and mosaics, often bring stories to life and depict variants to the myths we know from literature. Susan Woodford's *Images of Myths in Classical Antiquity* (Cambridge: Cambridge University Press, 2003) will help you learn to recognize myths in ancient art; her focus is on Greek vase painting. T. H. Carpenter's *Art and Myth in Ancient Greece* (London: Thames & Hudson, 1991) covers vase painting by theme and character. For a broader introduction to classical art, try Mary Beard and John Henderson's *Classical Art: From Greece to Rome* (Oxford: Oxford University Press, 2001). For myths in art from the Middle Ages to the present, see Lucia Impelluso's wonderfully compact *Gods and Heroes in Art* (Los Angeles: J. Paul Getty Museum, 2003). Philip Mayerson's *Classical Mythology in Literature, Art, and Music* (Newburyport, Mass.: Focus, 2001) is a generous survey of the lasting impact of myth in the West.

ACKNOWLEDGMENTS

Thanks, first and foremost, to Amy Treadwell, my editor, from whose suggestion this book sprang. I also wish to thank design director Aya Akazawa and illustrator Tinou Le Joly Senoville for their enthusiasm and dedication. I am indebted to John G. Pedley, Professor Emeritus of Classical Archaeology and Greek at the University of Michigan, for his careful reading and critical eye. Thanks also go to Keith Buckingham, Graham Hewson, Alison Rush, Noël Schiller, and Jim and Erin Vito for their patience and innumerable suggestions.

INDEX

CONVERSION CHART

For gods and heroes

GREEK	ROMAN
Aias	Ajax
Apollo	(same)
Aphrodite	Venus
Ares	Mars
Artemis	Diana
Asclepius	Aesculapius
Athena	Minerva
Demeter	Ceres
Dionysus	Bacchus (or Liber Pater)
Eos (Dawn)	Aurora
Eris (Strife)	Discordia
Eros	Cupid (or Amor)
Hades	Pluto (or Dis Pater)
Helios (the Sun)	(same)
Hephaestus	Vulcan
Hera	Juno
Heracles	Hercules
Hermes	Mercury
Hestia	Vesta
Odysseus	Ulixes (or Ulysses)
Pan	Faunus
Persephone (or Kore, "girl")	Proserpina
Poseidon	Neptune
Zeus	Jupiter (or Jove)